The Weekend Captain's Guide to Basic Boating

The Weekend Captain's Guide to Basic Boating

Captain Jeffrey Caso

Library of Congress Number:		2003091681
ISBN:	Hardcover	1-4134-0129-5
	Softcover	1-4134-0128-7

This is a work of fiction. Names, characters, places and incidents
either are the product of the author's imagination or are used
fictitiously, and any resemblance to any actual persons, living or
dead, events, or locales is entirely coincidental.

This book was printed in the United States of America.

To order additional copies of this book, contact:
Xlibris Corporation
1-888-795-4274
www.Xlibris.com
Orders@Xlibris.com
18406

Contents

FOR MY WIFE LYNN
AND MY THREE SONS WHO
CONSISTENTLY SUPPORT ME IN
ALL OF MY ENDEAVORS.

PREFACE

As boaters, we all share certain experiences which make our hobby at times unpleasant. Every boater has had difficulty with boat handling, has run aground or has had an on the water breakdown. These problems are universal. That is, they happen to each and every boater, whether he cares to admit it or not. Countering these problems is our love for the water which is the reason why we do what we do.

Such negative experiences deprive us of the rejuvenating action that boating provides and create stress. Today, both at home and at work, stress is unfortunately ever present. We have chosen boating as our release. It is a powerful, medicinal pursuit which has the ability to heal our souls. However, when we experience problems, we feel wronged. In addition, it creates feelings of disappointment and embarrassment which eventually lead to a loss of self confidence.

Knowledge, preparedness and ultimately experience will be what gets us through the rough spots. I have spent a great deal of time sorting through the volumes of material out there. I have discarded the impertinent and kept the important information that you need to have as general knowledge. Additionally, by choosing to learn from the mistakes that I have made, I can pass along this hard won information so that you do not need to learn the difficult way. In essence, I will teach you the safe proven way. This will give you the confidence that you need to enjoy your chosen, albeit potentially dangerous hobby.

All we really want is to have fun, so that we can recharge ourselves. We want to enter the more stressful parts of our lives in a better frame of mind. This will make us happier, more productive, better people. By having good old fashioned fun, armed with the knowledge you need to do it correctly, the rest will follow on its own. Enjoy it and safe boating.

CHAPTER 1

WHAT IS IT?

Everything should be made as simple as possible . . .
but not simpler.

—Albert Einstein

A complete understanding of your boat, whether it is a 14 foot skiff or a 50 foot trawler, is paramount to success. I do not mean the intricate physics of boat design or the interactions of buoyancy and gravity, but basically what your boat will and will not do in a given situation. You need to know what you can call upon it to do, so you get a safe and appropriate response. First, I feel that it is imperative to review some of the parts of your boat so that when you are dealing with people in the boating business, or even other boaters, you know the language so you can talk the talk. Remember, the people you will be dealing with may be quick to judge you, especially if they are in the industry. You want to be knowledgeable and confident and they will respect you for it.

Lets start at the dock, your boat is tied up stern to.

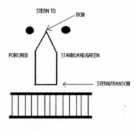

The portion of your boat closest to the dock is the **transom,** or the rearmost terminus of the boats hull. Facing the **bow,** or most forward end of your boat, the **port side** is to your left and is marked with a red sidelight. The **starboard side** is to the right and is marked with a green sidelight. Standing in the boat, forward of the transom, you are on the **sole,** which is the floor of the **cockpit** or the open space usually in the **aft,** or most sternward section of the boat. The sole is also the floor of the **cabin,** which is the inside portion of the boat if it has one. You walk forward to the **helm,** the place from which you drive. Depending upon the boat, this may be **amidships** or the center of the boat. It may also be to starboard. There may even be more than one station from which to pilot the boat.

Your boat has other dimensions which we are also interested in because they do invariably come up in conversation and remember, we want you to be well versed in all aspects of your boat. The boat's greatest length is often referred to as **LOA** or **length overall.** The **beam** is the greatest width of the boat. The **gunwales** (pronounced gunnels) are the top of the hulls sides and basically they run up both the port and starboard sides from stern to bow. The distance from the gunwales to the water is called the **freeboard.** This measurement is important because if the freeboard is low, meaning the gunwale is close to the water, the boat may be in danger of being swamped by a wave. The freeboard may be low because of the design of the boat. Such is the case in many small skiffs, or it may be so because the boat is dangerously overloaded with gear or people. You should make a mental note of how the boat looks as she sits in the water, basically unloaded. Then, if as you load her up she loses an excessive amount of freeboard, the gunwales become too close to the water and you are in serious danger of being swamped and sinking.

The next dimension is also very important, it is the deepest depth of the boat below the waterline, including anything that hangs below the hull, such as the engine, rudder, prop etc. It is the boats **draft,** which is also the measurement of the shallowest water the boat can navigate through without running aground. For small boats, add an imaginary 6" to the actual draft and for larger boats you may want to add up to two imaginary feet as a safety factor. Remember, the draft of the boat can change with the amount of people and gear in it. This is to say, as freeboard decreases the draft increases. Keeping this in mind will allow you to easily calculate your draft by looking at your freeboard. Your average draft can easily be found while at dockside. Set up the boat with your usual gear and number of persons. Then determine the deepest part of the boat, usually the propeller, keel or the **skeg** which is the piece of metal just below the propeller. Use a tape measure to measure from the waterline to this deepest object. Add at least 6" or any number you feel comfortable with as a safety factor and make a note of this. Now, whenever you go out, add to this number if you increase the number of people on board or your amount of gear. Use your freeboard, or lack of, to assist you in finding a draft for that day. Make sure that you are comfortable with this depth. I never do the reverse, I never subtract from my average draft. If I go out lighter, I prefer to err on the side of safety. People may ask "How much does she draw?" The question actually is; What is the boats draft? Its pretty basic, but sometimes a source of confusion.

There are a just a few more important terms that we can run through quickly before moving on. The **bilge** is the lowest internal portion of the hull. That is why water tends to accumulate there. The **keel** on the other hand is the lowest external portion of the hull. It can take on many different shapes and in the case of a flat bottomed boat, it may not be present at all. **Chines** are the lines where the bottom and sides of the hull meet and the term **deadrise** is the angle of the hull made by the keel up to the chine. The deadrise, measured in degrees, will usually change from bow to stern.

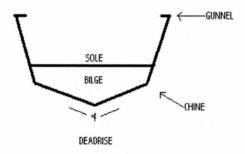

The type of hull you have is also very important. There are two basic classifications. First, there are displacement hulls which basically push their way through the water as they go.

Second, there are planing hulls, which are more commonly found on recreational boats. They begin as displacement hulls, pushing water as they go, but as they approach a critical speed, the hull begins to rise out of the water and planes. That is, only a portion of the hull remains in the water at this critical speed, reducing friction, allowing the hull to move along more efficiently.

Hulls can take on many shapes as well. The simplest design is the flat bottom, which is a fairly stable design at rest.

Underway, the flat bottomed hull almost slaps at the water and at times can really pound. Conversely, the vee bottom hull tends to cut through the water and therefore, offers less pounding while underway.

If the vee is very pronounced or strong, this type of hull can be less stable or tend to roll side to side at rest. A modified vee hull generally flattens out as you approach the stern. This gives you both a vee at the bow for cutting through the chop and a flat stern for stability while at rest. Keeping the shortfalls of each type of hull in mind, designers pick and choose the best features of each and have developed many hybrids as well as multi-hull designs of all shapes and sizes. Power catamarans, one such result of this picking and choosing, have gained popularity and offer both a smooth ride and stability while at rest. They may look odd with their high sides and they usually require the use of two outboards. In boat design, there seems to be a give and take between function and appearance.

Manufacturers also offer many different power choices to help confuse us even more. We will go through each choice and discuss the pros and cons of each. Learning a little bit about each type of engine gives you a greater awareness of what is out there running next to you. This will help you to understand each engines capabilities and limitations. Remember, knowledge is confidence and that is what we want most. The four basic choices of power are inboard, outboard, stern drive (inboard/outboard) and jet drives. There are other types of propulsion available. We will however, limit our discussion to these most common forms.

Inboard engines are basically a marine version of an automobile engine, usually of four, six or eight cylinders. They may run on gasoline or diesel fuel. Diesel engines are typically very strongly built, reliable engines that can easily stand up to many hours of hard use. They are usually more economical to run than gasoline engines. For these reasons they are the first choice for commercial vessels, whose captains rely upon them for their livelihood and also their safety. Diesel fuel is also thought of as being safer than gasoline and less likely to explode. Indeed it is at room temperature, but in a fire, if diesel is heated above its flash point of 100 degrees Fahrenheit it also will give off flammable vapor. This vapor packs an even greater punch than gasoline when it explodes. Just so you know, the flash point of gasoline is -45 degrees Fahrenheit and therefore can explode at virtually any temperature we may practically encounter. Be careful with both fuels and do not think that diesel is unable to cause a fire.

Gasoline engines are more commonplace among pleasure boaters. They are less expensive than diesel, can be repaired by more mechanics and gasoline in some areas is much easier to find than diesel fuel. When properly maintained and used correctly, they can also be very safe.

The inboard engine is mounted in the deepest recesses of the boat called the engine compartment. In small to mid sized boats, the engine may actually be mounted backwards to allow it to be placed as far aft as possible. This type of installation requires the use of a Vee drive to redirect the propeller shaft sternward and through the hull at an angle conducive to good performance. A transmission is also necessary to allow shifting between forward, neutral and reverse. The propeller shaft goes through the hull and is turned by the engine. This in turn moves the propeller which causes a circular movement of water called the propeller wash. This rotating swirl of water moves the boat forward. A rudder is mounted aft of the propeller and when moved by the steering wheel, sits at various angles to the propeller wash.

In doing so, it redirects the flow of water and causes the boat to turn. A feature unique to inboard powered boats is that because the rudder is placed aft of the propeller, when the boat is operating in reverse, the rudder is rendered somewhat useless. This happens because the propeller wash is not going past the rudder and therefore you have very little control. The operator can however, take advantage of the propellers torque, which tends to cause the boat to swing to port or to starboard depending upon the particular boat and the direction of the propellers movement. This swinging must be known by the operator as a characteristic of this boat and planned for ahead of time.

The propeller shaft, propeller and rudder is collectively known as the running gear and usually hangs down below the boats hull. It is critical to the successful operation of these boats that they do not come in contact with the bottom at any time. Grounding, even lightly, can cause the skeg or the metal member that holds the rudder in place, to be damaged or torn off. The prop can also be damaged and the propeller shaft bent.

Any of these problems will require a tow and having the boat hauled for an expensive repair. The worst case scenario is that the boat can be in danger of sinking if this running gear is torn off. For this reason, these boats are generally big water boats and are not practical for shoal areas or areas with low water and ever changing channels due to rapidly moving sand.

These engines as stated earlier are marinized automobile engines. That is, they have a fresh water cooling system consisting of a water pump and a series of hoses which carry antifreeze and water through and around the engine. They do not however, have a radiator to exchange the engines heat with the outside air. Instead they use a raw water or sea water heat exchanger that employs the use of a separate water pump which operates off of the engines fan belt. It pumps cool sea water into the heat exchanger which removes the engines heat from the fresh water system. This cooled mix of water and antifreeze is then returned to the engine to once again begin to gather heat and perform its task all over again. The now hot, raw water is expelled through the boats exhaust system and back into the surrounding water. It is important to note that these two systems, fresh and raw, are entirely separate. They are only mixed during a serious problem with the engines system. Raw water moving through the engine itself will quickly cause corrosion, clog the engine block and lead to catastrophic failure.

Winterization of these engines is extensive. Each individual system must be addressed. The fuel system needs to be stabilized. The raw water system needs to be drained and protected with antifreeze. The fresh water system needs to be protected with the proper mix of antifreeze and water. This should be left to the pros, if you are not fully comfortable with doing it yourself. One small mistake or omission could easily lead to a freeze up and a ruptured heat exchanger, a damaged exhaust system or a cracked engine block.

The next class of motors are Outboards.

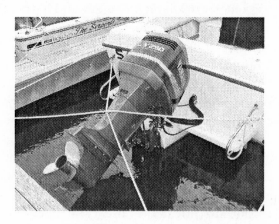

They are self contained units hung on the boats transom and are hugely popular for many reasons. One primary reason is that they can be manually or automatically tilted out of the water and grounding, while it is important to avoid, is no longer such a big event. If the lower unit of the outboard contacts the bottom, the engine can simply be shut down and tilted up to prevent damage. If however, the grounding is severe, the power tilt and trim feature can be damaged and require repair.

Outboard motors are cooled very simply with only one system, a raw water system. Sea water is pumped through the engines water jacket or the internal spaces surrounding the parts of the engine that get hot. Heat is exchanged in those spaces from the hot engine to the cool sea water. The heated sea water is expelled two ways. First, through the exhaust system and out the prop hub or the center of the propeller. Second and more importantly, excess water is discharged out the back of the engine in a noticeable or telltale stream of water.

This stream should be checked every time the engine is started to assure that the water pump is working properly. At idle or when running slowly on some boats you can actually hear this stream hitting the water and a visual check is not always necessary. If you cannot hear it however, make sure you look for it.

The outboard motor's water pump works by means of an impeller spinning directly on the engines drive shaft. The impeller or rubber portion of the pump which moves the water, requires maintenance and changing according to the manufacturer's recommendations. A broken or bad impeller will decrease or stop the flow of water through the engine. This will cause the engine to overheat, usually sounding an alarm. Immediately, you should look for that telltale stream of water exiting the engine. If it is not present, shut the engine down or the excessive heat could cause the engine to seize. A seized engine is when the internal temperature becomes so great that the pistons melt and fuse themselves to the walls of the cylinders in which they move. Other catastrophic breakage of parts ensues and usually the engine can never be run again. For this reason it is important to change the impeller when suggested. Most boat owners will change it every year as a precaution. It should not be very expensive to do so. Also, just as important, is to watch the raw water intake ports which are a series of holes in the engines lower unit. These can get clogged by seaweed, litter (plastic bags especially) or even barnacles. You should familiarize yourself with this area and if an overheat alarm sounds you should shut down, tilt the engine and check this intake for an obstruction. A small wire should be kept onboard to probe the holes because sometimes, especially after a grounding, the obstruction could be sand, packed into the intake. Be careful when doing this in open water. If you cannot identify an obstruction or the sea conditions make it too dangerous to safely check, then just drop anchor if you can and call for a tow. A trick commonly used, is if you feel that you may have driven through a load of seaweed or litter and then you get an overheat alarm, slow down and move to a safe area so you do not become a hazard to other boaters. Shift into neutral and then quickly reverse the engine for just a few seconds. This will sometimes clear an obstruction. You will know the obstruction is cleared if you now see that telltale stream of water coming from the back of the engine. If you do not see the water stream and the alarm continues to sound, shut down right away. If you try this, do not dilly dally. Do it fast and definitively. You do not have much time.

While we are on the subject of outboard maintenance, proper lubrication is the key to long engine life, not to mention reliability. There are two areas where lubrication is necessary. The lower unit is one. The lower unit is the portion of the motor below the powerhead, all the way down to the propeller. The gear oil in the lower unit needs to be changed regularly, according to the manufacturers suggestions. Most people like to do it yearly under normal use. Again it is another fairly inexpensive bit of preventative maintenance. It is important for the obvious reason of replacing spent oil for better lubrication, but also for diagnostic purposes. When you look at the old oil, it tells you a lot about how well your engines functioning. Specifically, the condition of the oil seals which are supposed to separate the gear oil from the raw water of the engines cooling system and the surrounding water. Leakage of water into the oil makes the oil milky white and it means you have to find the source of the leak or you could destroy the lower unit. Also, metal filings in the oil could indicate a problem with the way the gears are meshing or a shifting problem that can be addressed early on. Later detection of these problems obviously will cost you more to repair them. More importantly it may save you from a breakdown on the water.

The second area where proper lubrication is critical is the walls of the engines cylinders. This allows the engines pistons to work more efficiently and smoothly, therefore decreasing heat buildup. A lack of proper lubrication in this area is another way the engine can overheat and possibly seize. To discuss the ways in which this area is lubricated, we must first learn about the fuel the engine uses.

Almost all outboards are gasoline powered. Every once in a while you will hear about a company that makes a diesel outboard. For our purposes, we really only need to know that they exist, but they are rare birds that we will probably never see. Two stroke gasoline engines require that oil is mixed with the gasoline. It can be done manually by directly pouring the oil into the fuel tank, or the engine may be oil injected. This means that there is a tank or reservoir where two cycle oil is placed. It is drawn into the engine and mixed as the gasoline is used. This system is easy, as no calculations are necessary to assure a proper mixture. Therefore, no mistakes can be made which will cause the engine to run improperly.

Using too much oil causes a heavy bluish exhaust and fouled spark plugs. Using too little oil may cause the engine to run hot and may even cause the engine to seize. Just remember, if your engine is oil injected, top off the reservoir whenever you fuel up. Also, carry a pint or two of oil with you in case your reservoir runs empty or for some reason your oil injection system fails. In the event of a failure, you can simply add oil directly into your fuel tank at the proper ratio and thereby override the oil injection system. With a newer outboard, you may be alerted to an oil injector malfunction by a warning light on the dash, an audible alarm or your engine may automatically decrease its speed in an attempt to avoid a seize up. Keep your manual handy to be able to identify what each alarm may mean. It can be pretty confusing when an alarm sounds. Another way to possibly tell if your oil injection system has failed, is if the engine overheats even while your water pump is working properly. You can confirm your pump is operational by that good old telltale stream of water exiting the back of the engine. There are dozens of other reasons for your engine to overheat while your water pump is operating properly, other than just a failed oil injection system. However, just about the only thing you can possibly do on the water to correct the problem is to suspect this system. The worst thing that could happen is that your engine runs with too much oil until you dilute the ratio back down by adding more fuel to the tank. If you find yourself in a situation where you need to add oil directly to the fuel tank, you must first know the proper ratio for your engine as specified in your owners manual. The usual ratios are either 50:1 or 100:1. For example, 50:1 means that for every fifty ounces of gas, you add one ounce of oil or for every fifty gallons of gas, you add one gallon of oil etc. You figure out the amount of gas you have by using the fuel gauge and knowing the size of the tank. Then extrapolate the amount of oil necessary. Remember 1 gallon = 128 ounces. It is this oil that lubricates the walls of the engines cylinders, allowing it to run efficiently and without problems.

There is another way that a cylinders walls can be lubricated. It is with a different type of system entirely, called a four stroke engine. That is, one which carries its own oil in a closed system much like your car. It therefore requires no mixing of gas and oil. Because no oil is burned in the cylinders, as in a two stroke engine, these newer four stroke engines emit less pollutants into the surrounding air and water. They are also quieter engines on the whole. For these reasons they are environmentally more friendly. When they become more widespread in manufacture, their price will also come down and they will become more competitive with their two stroke relatives. As this happens, regulations will probably require them to replace two strokes altogether and rightfully so. We need to take steps today to ensure clean waterways for our children. Other than checking and changing the oil, these outboards operate much the same as other outboards.

Just a few more points need to be made about outboard motors to be complete in our discussion. A fantastic feature of outboards when used properly, is power tilt and trim. By use of a switch usually located on the throttle lever, the engine, if so equipt, can be tilted up and out of the water (only while not running). Additionally, the fore and aft position of the boat or the attitude can be corrected for while underway. From time to time, due to the weight distribution of gear or people, the bow may tend to sit lower in the water than usual. This may make the boat have difficulty getting up on plane. As the bow is plowing through the water, you can trim the engine out a bit, which will make the bow rise and compensate for this improper weight distribution. Conversely, if the excess weight is in the stern, the boat will squat a bit aft and the bow will be up. By trimming the engine in, the bow will come down and the stern will lift. This is a great feature and will allow the boat to operate properly under many conditions. We will discuss this more later.

Probably the biggest advantage of the outboard powered boat is its extremely responsive steering. Because the entire engine swings when moved by the steering wheel, the propellers thrust is so directed that the boat moves sharp and fast. Also, when operating in reverse, the movement of the engine, in addition to the pull of the propeller which is spinning in reverse, moves the boat quite efficiently.

Winterization of the outboard motor is also very easy. With the engine sitting vertically and out of the water, the raw cooling water drains out by itself. It is good to flush the raw water system with clean water to remove salt and sediment according to the recommendations of the manufacturer. This can be done in many ways. The easiest of which is to use a set of motor flushers. They look like ear muffs and go over the water intake ports. Some engines have a fitting which allows a garden hose to be connected directly to the engine. A word of caution is to stand clear of the engine while it is running and never attempt to shift it into gear. A spinning propeller anywhere, but especially out of water can be lethal.

The gear oil should be changed and the water pump impeller should also be changed if necessary. The engine should also be fogged, which means a lubricating spray is applied into the intake manifold where it is distributed throughout the engine and protects the metal surfaces during the winter lay up. Also, keep in mind that all outboards, especially smaller ones, are subject to theft. Keep them in a safe place and always lock them up.

After learning a bit about inboard engines and outboard engines we now come to an interesting hybrid, the inboard/outboard, I/O or stern drive.

Like the inboard, the engine is mounted inside the boat just forward of the transom. Outside the boat, there is the outdrive which resembles the lower unit of an outboard. This class of engines tries to combine the best features of both types of engines previously discussed. Stern drives generally run on gasoline and are four stroke engines. That is, it is not necessary to mix oil with the gasoline. They are lubricated by a separate closed system which must be checked regularly and kept full. They are either fresh water cooled with a separate raw water system which employs the use of a heat exchanger or they may be only raw water cooled like an outboard. Fresh water cooling is advantageous, as only a mix of fresh water and anti freeze passes through the engines internal spaces. Raw or seawater in these spaces can cause scaling and salt deposits to form making cooling less effective. Currently, there is a new diesel model which touts both reliability and fuel economy. The future looks bright for this stern drive as several large boat builders are offering it as an option.

Outside the boat we have an outdrive which gives us the advantage of power tilt and trim and all of the benefits that go along with it. This includes being able to tilt the outdrive almost all the way out of the water. We also have the maneuverability of an outboard, where the steering wheel moves the entire outdrive and directs the propeller wash to move the boat accordingly. We also have better responsiveness operating in reverse.

With all these advantages you would think there would be no need for any other type of engine. We will discuss the few disadvantages next, but I guess the reason why stern drives do not have a lock on the market share is that people like each particular type of engine for their specific needs and are generally very partial to their choice.

As far as I can see, the main disadvantage of stern drives is that they take up quite a bit of space in the boat itself. In a larger boat this is not such a big deal; but in a smaller boat, this starts to become significant. Mechanically, there are quite a few parts that are unique to these designs which involve the mating of the inboard and the outboard components. The more parts, especially specialized parts, the more chance for problems and the more difficult it may be to find a mechanic to deal with them. Also, the water pump for the raw water system is located in the outdrive in all but a few of these engines and the boat will require hauling if a problem arises. In most installations, the outdrive cannot be fully tilted out of the water. This is important when the boat sits idle for a while, especially in warmer climates. Growth of algae and barnacles can clog water intakes and cause general mayhem with the lower unit. Additionally, winterization of these engines is extensive and best left to the pros. Another problem is theft and may only apply to various localities. In my area, the day the boat is hauled for the winter is the day the outdrive needs to be removed.

It seems as though they are hot commodities and are stolen very quickly. Removing them is a hassle, but it needs to be done for the winter anyway. It also makes for a long day in the spring, especially if you hang your own outdrive. It will need to be hung and launched the same day. You can always tell when someone had trouble launching right away when you see a car parked right up against the drive. To remove the drive you need to back it out several inches and with the car in the way this is impossible. I suppose these thugs could just steal the car first if they were smart enough to think of it.

Another problem which affects outdrives or any metal below the waterline such as rudders, struts, propellers or thru hull fittings, is galvanic action or electrolysis. Galvanic action is a process caused by electrical current in the water. In the presence of an electrolyte or salty medium, less noble metals become anodes and lose free electrons. They are therefore wasted or lost causing them to become pitted, corroded and thinned. While more noble metals become cathodes which accept free electrons and are less adversely affected. This movement of electrons is essentially electricity and has a measurable voltage. In short, two dissimilar metals in a salty environment form a battery. When a battery goes dead and is unable to be recharged, the anode is totally gone or wasted, a slow process which takes place electron by electron. The greater the dissimilarity in the metals and the saltier the environment, the greater the electrical charge and the faster the wasting of the metal.

To protect your boat from galvanic action, the manufacturer strategically places Zincs or sacrificial anodes.

Zincs are very low on the nobility scale and therefore give up their electrons very easily. They are intentionally allowed to be wasted to protect the metals that we want, such as your outdrive or aluminum hull. Look at your Zincs at the end of a season and they certainly will not look like they did at the beginning of the season. Forget to change them for a season and they may even be entirely gone. Make sure that your yard changes them each and every season. You can change them yourself by matching up what you have at the boat supply store. They are usually screwed on and off with an Allen Key wrench.

In my other life as a Dentist, galvanic action is always of concern. When choosing restorations a dentist must consider what other metals are also present. Saliva makes a very good electrolyte for the transfer of electrons. Cases have been documented where inadvertently a gold onlay was placed in an upper tooth and a silver filling was in opposition below it. Whenever the patient bit down, the two dissimilar metals approached one another and a strong, painful shock occurred. I have seen situations where a gold restoration abutted a silver restoration and the silver corroded, pitted and failed prematurely. The silver, of course, being the less noble anode. Galvanic action is a very real problem.

Another source of stray electrical current surrounding a boat is found dockside. They may come from many sources, most commonly from improperly wired or poorly maintained shore side power outlets. They may also come from other boats that hookup to shore side power to keep their batteries charged or their refrigerators cold, where an onboard problem allows electricity to escape. An accelerated wasting of less noble metals takes place in these situations. Fish shaped or mermaid shaped Zincs on a chain are sold for added protection. You should drop one overboard, a foot or two deep, at your homeport or at any docks that you visit, if you feel as though there may be a problem. You need to keep an eye out for poor maintenance, a large number of boats hooked up to shore side power or other boats with these Zincs hanging off of their sides. A tester is available to check for proper wiring and is simple to use. You plug it into the outlet that you intend to use and an indicator light tells you if it is wired properly. At your home marina, if you notice a great deal of rapid wasting of your Zincs, talk to the marina staff. Correcting the problem could save you a bundle.

At the marina I keep my boat in, a friend who keeps his boat a few docks away, suffered such extreme electrolysis that you could punch a hole in his outdrive with only your finger. The entire drive needed to be replaced. That is why it is always a good idea to tilt your outboard or drive up as far as possible when not in use. It is good to know that situations like this commonly exist so that you can identify a problem long before it does expensive damage.

The final type of engine that we need to discuss is a relatively new design called a jet drive. Most commonly they are standard power on jet skis. This is because the operator is frequently in the water with the craft. These engines are safer under these conditions because they do not have a propeller which can do great harm to anyone that gets close. They derive their propulsive force from a powerful stream of water. This water can be directed to move the boat accordingly. A large intake port pulls seawater into a chamber where it is then forced out of the engine's drive. These gasoline engines can be in the form of an outboard or stern drive. They are generally two stroke, but can also be four stroke. Another advantage, beside safety, is that they are of greater use in extremely low or rocky water where a prop could easily be damaged. A disadvantage is in handling in close quarters. They require quite a bit of acquired skill to maneuver them accurately and smoothly.

What I have tried to accomplish in this chapter is to give

you a good understanding of your boat as well as other types of boats you may encounter. As you have probably noticed, I think its important for you to know the most common problems your engine might suffer. I feel that the cooling system is the most susceptible to problems which can cause the greatest damage regardless of engine type. You need to learn to be in tune with your gauges and spot problems early before they do great damage. Also, grounding is a common source of problems. In other sections, I will cover proper navigation to help you avoid low water in the first place. You must however, always be aware of minor signs and changes in the appearance of the water which may alert you to low water or underwater hazards. These signs may be a subtle change in the color of the water or a change on the surface such as rippling or breaking water. Always question any change and throttle back to give yourself time to evaluate what may be going on. I will also go into the need for a depth finder, even in a small boat, to use as an adjunct to good sense and observation. It is a necessary piece of equipment for safe boating.

Finally, I will teach you how and when to call for a tow and how to keep yourself and your passengers safe when you realize that you cannot go on. Many people get into trouble and cause more damage because their ego gets in the way. If you are overheating or suffering from an intermittent problem and presently you are in a stable situation; Why try to limp home? You run the risk of breaking down in an area that may be considerably more dangerous, not to mention the greater damage you may cause to your engine. Sit back, think about it and call for a tow from the safe spot, not when it becomes urgent and risky.

You will not be afraid to call for a tow after completing this book because you will have towing insurance through your local towing service or nationally, through Boat/US. This is so necessary. It is not expensive and it allows you to make a decision to call for a tow based upon your situation, not your pocketbook. It also gives you a great deal of confidence. You will be able to tell the towing service exactly where you are because you always carry a chart book of any area you may ever boat in. So there is no need to worry about causing confusion. You also have the know how and the means for calling for assistance, because you carry another piece of mandatory equipment, a VHF radio. We will also get into when to use the VHF and when to use the cell phone.

There is no stigma attached to being towed into port for any reason. I was once towed five miles into port when my engine lost power. I had my one year old son on board and when I quickly could not find the problem I called for the tow. Back in port, I realized the engines main grounding bolt had vibrated loose. After spending twelve cents on a lock washer, all was well again, but I never regretted my decision to call for the tow. My responsibility was to keep the situation safe and under control and that is what I did. As the captain of your boat, you have the same responsibility. Use the knowledge you have to keep things under control at all times.

Chapter 2

SHIP SHAPE

Take calculated risks.
That is quite different from being rash.
—General George S. Patton

B efore we should even attempt to leave the dock, we need to make sure we have the proper equipment on board so we can enjoy our hobby safely. Just as important as equipment, we need what most recreational boaters lack, that is the know how to use their safety equipment properly. In this section we will provide you with both the information you need to choose the proper equipment for your purposes and the knowledge you need to use this equipment to your advantage, whatever the situation may be. This will give you confidence, which is your most important asset when an emergency arises. I fully realize that this information as commonly presented can be somewhat boring. I take this section seriously because for me, boating is a family activity. When I put my wife and kids on board the game changes for me. I need to know that I have taken every precaution to ensure their safety.

The U.S. Coast Guard requires that we have certain safety equipment on board at all times. The list of necessary equipment changes according to the size of boat and type of engine. I feel this requirement is just a guide for us and really is what is minimally required. I will use their list, embellish upon it and offer suggestions for additional items. This entire compilation will be what I feel is realistically necessary to allow us to cope with whatever problem may arise.

I am reminded of a story about two men who worked in a marina. Every fall they would take a 14' work skiff out about one hundred yards off the marina to various moorings and tow back boats to haul them for the winter. This job became very routine, until one day when they got out just about to the mooring field and the engine cut out. After repeated attempts at restarting failed, they realized that the only things they had with them were the clothes on their backs. Drifting around on this cold and desolate October day, they were not reported missing until late that night when they failed to arrive home. The next day, they very fortunately were found by a fishing boat almost eleven miles out at sea. They were cold but otherwise unharmed. That is, I heard, until the Coast Guard got a hold of them. Supposedly, it took four hours for them to write up all the safety violations. Had the Coast Guard actually had the time to launch an extensive search for them, they might have also been responsible to pay for the cost of the search due to their gross negligence. Here's where a flare, a VHF radio, a float plan, an anchor etc. would have saved a lot of people a lot of aggravation. Plan for the best, but be prepared for the worst.

Lets start with the basics, The Coast Guard says that we need to have a Coast Guard approved Personal Flotation Device (PFD) for every person on board. PFD's are classified as Type I thru Type V. You could easily satisfy your Coast Guard requirement by purchasing the least expensive style, known as Type II's, to go around.

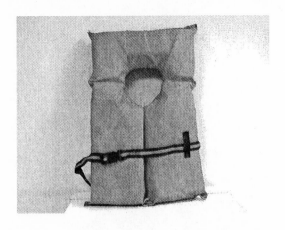

When you begin to learn the differences you may change your mind. Type II PFD's, probably the most common type found on recreational boats, slip over your head and have a strap that goes around your back. They cannot however be snugged up tightly around your body. For this reason they can slip and might not be able to keep your mouth above water. They are also less buoyant than other types and may not offer a larger wearer the flotation they need in many situations. Additionally, they may not be able to turn a wearer of any size face up in the water. This becomes important for two reasons. Firstly, if you find yourself in the water in an unconscious state, you may not be automatically turned face up. If you are lucky enough to be turned face up, you may not have the buoyancy you need to keep your mouth above water. Secondly, if you find yourself in the water for an extended period of time, you may become exhausted and again find it difficult to keep your mouth above water. If your boat came with a "Coast Guard Package" you can bet that the PFD's supplied were Type II's.

Type I PFD's are more like a vest which is worn rather than strapped on and while a little more expensive, offer you a great deal more.

They have more buoyancy and will turn most wearers face up in the water. They are therefore better at keeping your mouth above water. Look at it this way. Most adults do not wear PFD's all the time. If you find yourself in a situation where you do put one on, it is some sort of an emergency. When the situation becomes chaotic we do not just carefully slip into the water. We jump frantically from the boat in rough seas or are thrown from the boat. Usually other people on board are doing the same. In a situation like this, anything goes. Your head could contact a portion of the boat or debris in the water. Other people could land on you when they jump or are thrown in the water. In any situation, you run the risk of being knocked unconscious. Spending an extra twenty dollars on a Type I vest that will turn you face up at that critical moment seems like a bargain to me. This is one of those times where you not only get what you pay for, you get even more. Type II's have no place on my boat.

Keeping in mind that the best PFD is one that you will actually wear, I keep several inflatables on board.

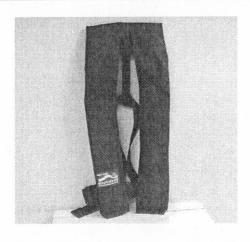

Many models are Coast Guard approved as Type V's, but only when worn. That means they must be on and buckled properly to count toward your requirement. They should only be considered for adults. In addition, I make sure to keep enough Type I's on board for everyone just in case. It is not required that Type I's be worn, only that there is one on board for each person on board. When it comes to inflatables, I prefer the manual/automatic suspender type vests, which means they will be inflated automatically by a disposable CO_2 cartridge as soon as you hit the water.

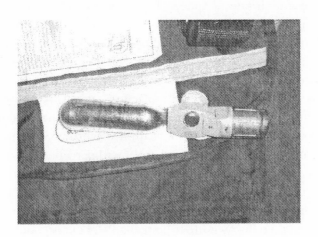

When inflated, they actually provide more buoyancy than a Type I and therefore are very good at keeping your mouth above water. They also will turn most wearers face up in seconds. When not inflated, they are comfortable to wear, not cumbersome and very cool on a hot day. They are required to have an indicator which shows that the CO_2 cartridge is installed properly, so there can be no mistakes. Manual versions are also available which require you to pull a ripcord to inflate it. This however, counts on the fact that you enter the water conscious and with enough presence of mind to pull the cord. I find the manual/automatic version to solve all the concerns I have. I leave them hanging on the back of my helm's chairs between outings and I use one all the time. I encourage my passengers to do the same. I also keep a few spare CO_2 cartridges and full rearming kits in a dry box on board and check the indicator on the vest every time I put it on to make sure it will work if I need it to.

A couple of years ago there was a seemingly strange incident that occurred in the waters off of Montauk, NY. One morning a large sportfishing boat was found wrecked on the rocks surrounding an island a few miles from the harbor. The hull was holed by the rocks and it appeared that the boat hit them at a high rate of speed. This was known by the extent of the damage to the hull, but also because both throttles were found to be 3/4 forward. The only other damage to the boat was a broken stern rail. The captain was never found. An investigation found that the captain was planning a big fishing trip the next day and took the boat out by himself to test out a few things, a kind of pre trip shakedown cruise. The evidence points to the captain, who at 3/4 throttle somehow lost his footing and fell overboard out the stern, breaking the rail in the process. The boat continued on until it met the rocks. This is a horrible event that could very well have ended differently. This guy may have had a fighting chance to save his own life if he had a PFD on. A good choice would have been an automatic inflatable vest. If you go out alone, put a vest on. Always. No exceptions. Boat size does not matter. Better yet, if you want to even have a shot at saving your boat, use a kill switch as well.

Most newer, small recreational boats are equipped with a device that can be attached to you, your clothes or your vest. If you fall overboard or move too far away from the helm, the engine is shut down. No matter what the size of your boat, if you do not have a kill switch, have your mechanic install one. Suppose for just a moment that you are out for a cruise and you take a larger wave than you are expecting. Sadly, you lose your footing and you are tossed overboard. Your vest inflates properly the instant you hit the water. You are not unconscious, but you failed to attach your kill switch lanyard to yourself and you are watching your boat speed away. That may very well be the best thing that could happen at that particular moment. Most boats, without a driver, will not just speed away. They usually will begin to circle. But guess what? You are invariably their target. You survive this surreal event, only to get clobbered by your own pride and joy. Wear the vest and the switch lanyard. If you do not have a switch, put one in. They are unbelievably inexpensive.

How about this scenario? You do everything right. You have the vest on and your kill switch shuts down the engine. You swim to the boat, but you find that you have no way to get back on board. Many a person has drowned by simply going for a swim, by falling in at the marina or believe it or not, every year loads of men fall overboard while attempting to urinate over the side. Once in the water, they realize they have no way to get back on board. If you do not have a swim platform and do not want one, a simple solution is folding steps. They are small, bolt onto the transom and fold out of the way when not in use. When needed, they give you just enough toe hold to hoist your exhausted self out of the water.

As I mentioned earlier, boating for me is a family activity. You will need to take special measures to ensure your child's safety. I look for several things when buying PFD's for my kids. Comfort is important because they are in them from the time they get out of the car in the marina parking lot to the time they get back to the car for the ride home. The vest should not be too tight, but not loose enough where it is able to be pulled off after being secured in place. You can test for this by placing the vest on as it would be worn on the water. Have the child raise their hands over their head. In this position, grab the vest at the shoulders and give it a good tug upward. If the vest wants to slide off over the child's head, it is too big or too loose. Vests are sized according to the weight of the child. This is a general guideline. The overriding factors to ensure a proper fit is that the vest should remain in place when pulled upward. It should feel comfortable and should look right when secured. PFD's are not like shoes. Never buy a size larger so the child can grow into it. It may be called upon to do its job while still big and not accomplish the desired goal.

In addition, for infants and toddlers, I want a grab strap on the collar to give me a positive hold. If I have a grab strap,

I definitely also want a leg strap which goes between their legs from the front to the back of the vest.

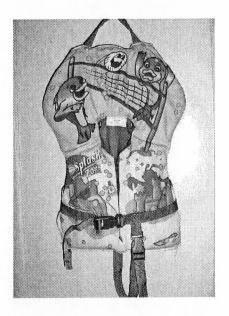

This keeps the vest from sliding off if you have to pull on the grab strap. The last thing you want to have happen is to pull them from the water and end up with only a vest in your hand because they slipped through, due to the fact that there was no leg strap; or worse, that it was not used. I also want them to be turned face up in the water and test this at home in our swimming pool. I stay close by to make sure it works as desired. Additionally, I like a bit of a vee neck design to give them more comfort at their neck. Some vests tend to be tight at the neck and that seems to be what my kids complain about the most. For us, boating is fun. If you do not want to wear the vest, you do not go and you miss the fun. We have no exceptions to this rule. I do however, try to find a vest that fits them well and one that has a fabric motif that they like. It just makes them happier. Most children's vests are classified as Type III Specialty Vests.

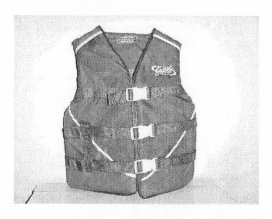

Keep in mind that there are also Type I vests for children that offer more security in offshore waters or rough seas. This is the only way to go if you are a blue water boater. There are also a few hybrid inflatable vests for children available. They have some foam floatation with manual/automatic inflation as an adjunct. I still feel, at this point in their development, that older may be better. I have not yet made the transition to these vests even though they boast being more comfortable. I was in a boat supply store one day and a fellow patron, who was also shopping for vests said, "Your going to spend fifty dollars on a vest for your kid?" My response was, well there were none for seventy five. This is not an area to cheap out. I once saw a sign in a motorcycle shop that said "If you have a ten dollar head, then buy a ten dollar helmet". I guess this idea is not unique to boating.

While we are on the subject of children, they also sell tethers which can be attached to the child's vest or to a special harness. I do not use them routinely, but I like to have them around in case you find yourself in rough seas or any other situation where you need to have a little more control over your child. I, however, never secure the tether to the boat itself. I only will attach it between my child and myself.

Just to be complete, some Type III PFD's are specialty items. Included in this group are manual inflatables and also PFD's with a specific uses. Some of these uses include waterskiing, jet skiing or as previously mentioned, children's vests. These commonly do not offer adequate flotation and generally may not be adequate in situations beyond what they were designed for. They also should only be used in situations where the likelihood of a fast rescue is great. Also in this group are flotation jackets which look much like a regular coat, but they are filled with foam flotation. A multitude of other versions exist. It is interesting to look around the various boat stores and see what is out there.

Type IV PFD's are throwable devices and are intended for man overboard situations. It is required that one be on board every boat over sixteen feet in length. I carry a couple and use them as seat cushions. I always have a polypropylene line tied onto at least one of them. Its use is limited if you throw it to someone, but do not have a way of pulling them back to the boat. Even better than these, are products made specifically for man overboard situations. One resembles a frisbee with a rope attached and can be thrown farther and more accurately than a cushion, even into a stiff wind. Another is actually classified as a type V PFD. It is called Life Sling and is deployed to help retrieve a person in the water. When the person in the water gets it, they place it over their head and under their arms. This facilitates retrieval back to the boat. It is mandatory equipment for anyone venturing offshore or engaging in activities which put them at risk for falling overboard. Having this on board does not fulfill your Coast Guard requirement for a PFD and both of these products may not fulfill your requirement for a Type IV.

There are many other products designed to help you out in man overboard situations. Only you know how far you need to take this issue to feel safe. Make sure you also have a plan to get a person back on board after they have gone over. Keep in mind, that due to the events of the situation, this person may be unconscious or otherwise unable to help you reboard him. Each boat is different. Some may be equipped for the use of a block and tackle, others you may need to get creative with. Planing ahead for this possibility is critical. If you do have to perform this operation, make sure you are wearing your PFD as well. If you operate your boat at night or even just want to feel safer you could attach strobe lights to each vest. Some people buy a roll of reflective tape and put it on each vest. Others will attach inexpensive light sticks, the kind you bend and they light up for several hours. I hear red is the easiest to see at night. Inexpensive signaling mirrors are a great adjunct as well. They clip on and do not rely on batteries or chemicals for their use. Plastic whistles, which will not rust, also cannot hurt. Think this through ahead of time for your situation and do what you need to do to make you feel safe. The key here is, do it. If you feel you need to, then go out and do it. Your first instincts are usually correct. Follow them.

The next and equally important required pieces of equipment you need to have onboard are fire extinguishers. The Coast Guard's requirement is really the bare minimum that you should venture out with. The Coast Guard classifies fire extinguishers as B-I or B-II. A B-I extinguisher has either 1.25 gallons of foam, 4 pounds of CO_2, or 2 pounds of dry chemicals. A B-II has 2.5 gallons of foam, 15 pounds of CO_2 or 10 pounds of dry chemical. For recreationally used boats, 16-26 feet in length, one USCG approved B-I is required. For 26-40 foot boats, two B-I's or one B-II are required. Finally, for those 40-65 feet, three B-I's or one B-I and one B-II are required. As you can well imagine, these requirements are less than minimal. They keep you within the law, but by no means safe in the event of a fire.

Let me tell you that probably one of the scariest sights to see is a burning boat.

Fire is serious anywhere, but on a boat with a limited amount of places to go and the fact that you are usually carrying a lot of fuel, it is downright fearsome. The days of wooden boats are waning and as you can imagine, wood is an obvious food for the fire. Well guess what? Fiberglass may take a little while to ignite, but when it does, it burns violently and gives off noxious fumes. Basically, we are taking our families out in a bomb. Realistically, you have only one defense once a fire breaks out and not much time.

The National Fire Protection Association (NFPA) has issued fire extinguisher recommendations which go beyond the Coast Guards. Their suggestions for location and number is shown in Table 1.

NFPA Fire Extinguisher Recommendations

Type of Boat	# of Extinguishers	Location
Open Outboard	2	Helm and Cockpit
Outboard Cruiser	2	Helm and Galley
Runabouts	2	Helm and Cockpit
Cruisers Under 26'	2	Helm and Galley
Cruisers 26'-40'	3	Engine Compartment, Helm, Galley
Cruisers 40'-65'	4	Engine Compartment, Helm, Galley And Crew's Quarters
Sailboats under 26'	2	Companionway and Forward Hatchway
Sailboats 26'-40'	3	Companionway or Helm, Galley or Outside Engine Compartment, And Forward Hatchway
Sailboats 40'-65'	4	Companionway or Helm, Galley or Outside Engine Compartment, Crew's Quarters, And Forward Hatchway

A good rule of thumb is that you should not have to travel more than half of the boat's length to reach one. In addition, you need to have the proper class of extinguisher for the type of fire that you have. This is easily remedied by getting only tri-class or ABC extinguishers. Nobody can remember each classification of fire and why even try? Cover yourself for all possibilities with an ABC extinguisher which is marked U.S. Coast Guard Approved. To be complete, I will go through the classification of fires here. If you are properly equipped, there is no need to commit them to memory. Class A fires are ordinary combustibles: wood, paper, cushions, fiberglass, canvas etc. Class B fires are flammable liquids: gasoline, propane, diesel, oil, paint etc. Class C fires are electrical in nature: wiring, machinery etc.

The NFPA goes even further in its recommendations for dealing with on board fires. Firstly, they say you should decide if you should even attempt to fight the fire yourself. Of course, your thinking that you are definitely going to save your vessel. Well think about it this way. You should spend the critical few seconds you have, after a fire breaks out, deciding if you have a chance at containing the fire. If you have even the slightest doubt, do not even try. Radio for help before the fire burns through the battery cables. This includes notifying someone, preferably the Coast Guard, of your situation and location. If fiberglass begins to burn, remember it is extremely hot and gives off noxious fumes. You need to get off the boat immediately. Fight the fire, if and only if, it is small and confined to the area it started. Generally, if you do not get to it in two minutes you are too late. Fight it if you have a way out and can keep your back to the exit and are confident that you can operate the extinguisher effectively. This includes aiming the nozzle at the base of the fire. Hold the extinguisher upright, sweep from side to side at the base of the fire or use a series of short blasts. Check for glowing embers and repeat if a flashback occurs. Keep in mind that an extinguisher can be fully discharged in under 10 seconds. Therefore you will need to use it sparingly and have a backup or two.

The only thing I would add, is to immediately prepare your passengers for whatever may arise by having them put on their PFD's when the problem first arises. Also, I feel its important to get a feel for the cause of the fire because this may assist you in putting it out by stopping its fuel supply. The location of the fire helps to determine its cause. If the fire is in or near the engine its cause may be fuel or electrical. Shut the engine or engines down immediately and turn the key all the way to the off position to stop the flow of electricity. If easily accessible, shut the flow of fuel down from the tanks. You do not want to open up the engine compartment up right away because you might be feeding oxygen to the fire and making things worse. If you have planned ahead with an inboard or stern drive you should have installed fire ports. They are under ten dollars, can be installed easily and allow you to spray a fire extinguisher into the engine compartment without opening the hatch. If the fire is located at the helm it is probably electrical. You should have a battery switch located somewhere near the battery. Turn this switch to the off position right away. If the fire is located in the galley, it is probably related to whatever fuel you carry to operate your stove. Alcohol is the most common, but some boats carry propane. If its propane, shut the tank immediately. Then deal with the fire.

To recap, have the proper number and size of fire extinguishers for all type of fires. They will be marked ABC. Using the parameters described, decide if you should even begin to fight the fire. Call for help early, while you still have power and prepare your passengers by making sure they are wearing PFD's. If you are going to fight the fire, discharge your extinguisher as suggested, preferably in short bursts. Then reevaluate the situation and make sure the fire does not restart. To help with this, try to determine it's cause and shut down its fuel source. Make a decision as to the seaworthiness of the vessel and the situation you are in. If the boat is adrift and at risk of collision or grounding, you may need to drop the anchor. If other boats are standing by and sea conditions permit, it may be safer to board another boat. The key here to help you is to keep the Coast Guard advised of the situation. They will advise you of what to do. They will know how far away help is, so just keep them informed and remember they are the professionals and they are there to help you.

Basic maintenance on your fire extinguishers is very important also. Check both the extinguisher and the mounting bracket monthly for rust or signs of damage. If the mounting bracket is made of metal, make sure it is operable and keep it lubricated. Check the gauge on the extinguisher to make sure it is fully pressurized. Keep them clean so they are ready if you need them. I also take them out of the bracket at least twice a year and turn them upside down several times to make sure the powder inside has not clumped together on the bottom. Replace or recharge any extinguishers that have been used, even if it is only partially spent. Remember also to put the extinguisher back into the bracket. Many extinguishers only fulfill your Coast Guard requirement if they are in the bracket.

Because the VHF radio plays such a vital role in an emergency situation, I will diverge from Coast Guard requirements to discuss some of the details of the VHF radio and its use. While it is not a required piece of equipment for many non-commercial vessels, it is highly recommended and I would not leave the dock without one. An FCC ship's station licence is not required for non-commercial vessels under 65 feet since 1996. That alone makes having one so much easier. You must still abide by the FCC's operating rules and we will cover these as we go on.

You must be aware that a VHF radio's ability to send and receive messages is basically by what is termed "line of sight". What this means is that the radio's signal, both in and out, is in a straight line. Anything in the way of this line will interfere with the signal. This means that land masses, other boats, waves and even the earth's curvature will decrease the distance you can send and receive messages. Therefore, to maximize your range, the antenna should be as long as practical and placed as high as possible on your boat. This will increase your line of sight. The antenna itself will also have a rating of what is termed "gain". Gain, measured in decibels or db, is the antenna's ability to amplify the signal, either in or out. Without getting into the minutia of this rating, remember the higher the gain the longer the range. Because things can never be that easy, it is necessary to add that as the gain increases the signal becomes more narrowly focused and can cause problems with reception in heavy or rolling seas. The bottom line is for our purposes, inshore or near coastal, 6 db is good 8 db is better.

Interestingly, several other factors will affect your radio's range. Briefly, they are the length of the antenna's cable, which gives us a power loss over its length, so the shorter the better with the fewest bends or kinks. A high quality shielded cable is best, with a good connector for uniting the cable and the radio. Several precautions are necessary to prevent any water intrusion into the cable. They include sealing any nicks in the cable immediately and using heat shrink tubing or electrical tape at the junction between the cable and the connector.

Now that you are set up correctly, you have a great resource at your finger tips. Using it properly is really easy. Do not be afraid of it. The next few paragraphs will help you to understand what it is all about, so it will be demystified and therefore you will feel more comfortable in using it. So lets get started.

The U.S. Coast Guard monitors channel 16 all day, every day, all year. Channel 16 is designated as the distress, urgency, safety, calling and replying channel for all vessels. This includes both commercial and private vessels. What this means, is that you can use channel 16 to call or hail another vessel or to contact the Coast Guard to report an emergency, an urgent or an unsafe situation. Once contact is established you must switch channels to conduct your conversation. This helps to keep channel 16 clear for others. Recently, channel 9 has been designated as a hailing channel for non-emergencies. This is an attempt to move some of the traffic or usage off of channel 16. The Coast Guard however, may not monitor channel 9 and they want you to conduct any calls concerning distress, urgency and safety only on channel 16. Table 2 gives you a listing of the available channels and their intended uses. You will notice that the channels designated as recreational working channels are the ones we should switch to after establishing contact with our intended party on channel 16.

Table 2

Channel 16- For Hailing, Safety or Emergency use only

Channel 9- Pleasure boat Hailing

Channel 6- Inter ship safety communications

Channels 68,69,71,72,78- Working Channels for Recreational Boats. Use these to talk after hailing on channel 16 or 9

Channel 13- Ship to Ship Communications, usually commercial vessels. Use to request Bridge Openings in some areas

Channels 24,25,26,27,28,84,85,86,87- Used by Marine Operators

Channel 22- Coast Guard working channel. You will be alerted to switch to Channel 22 Alpha, after being alerted on Channel 16 that an emergency message will be broadcast.

Channels 1, 5, 12, 14, 20, 63, 65A, 66A, 73, 74, 77- Used for Port Operations, such as arranging docking in a transient marina.

Channel 70- Dedicated to Digital Selective Calling (DSC). DSC is an automated system that makes digital phone calls to report emergencies through our VHF Radio.

WX 1
WX 2- Weather Broadcasts, Receive Only
WX 3

So, to get started we will get really basic for a little bit. You should turn on your radio while at the dock. Set your volume level as desired and adjust the squelch properly. This is done by waiting for a break in any ongoing transmissions and then turning the squelch knob until the static is no longer heard. Then turn back the opposite way until you hear it, then just nudge the knob a bit the other way, until all is quiet.

This should give you a radio, free of interference with only the sound of clear voices being heard.

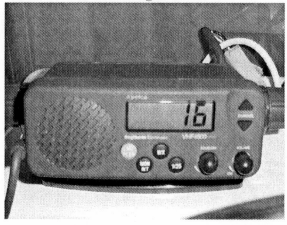

You will spend the majority of your time just listening to your radio. You are not required by law to have your radio turned on, but when it is on, you are required to monitor channel 16 when not using the radio for other purposes. These include listening to the weather report or talking on another channel. The reason you are required to monitor channel 16 is to help out in case of an emergency, such as hearing a distress call that others may have missed or hearing a call and finding that you may be close by to render assistance. The Coast Guard will announce any emergency weather information you may need such as an approaching thunderstorm on channel 16. You should also, prior to leaving the dock, listen to the radio's weather band for an updated forecast. They run continually and give a lot of pertinent information, such as wind speed and if it is increasing or decreasing, wave height and a prediction of the days weather. This includes the likelihood for storm formation or other severe weather.

Also on channel 16, The Coast Guard or other vessels may broadcast a warning about a hazard to navigation. Anytime an important message needs to be broadcast regarding a safety concern, it will be preceded by the word securitay (say-curitay) spoken three times and then the message. This is considered a third-priority message. Examples of messages you may hear are: "Securitay, Securitay, Securitay; Hello all stations; this is the United States Coast Guard Moriches Group with an emergency weather alert. All interested parties please change to channel Two-Two Alpha." You then change your radio to channel 22 and wait. You may then hear "Securitay, Securitay, Securitay. This is the United States Coast Guard Moriches Group with an emergency weather alert. The National Weather Service is reporting that a line of severe weather is approaching from the southwest at 15 knots. It is expected to cross over the Jones Inlet area in approximately 30 minutes. Wind gusts are expected to be in excess of 50 miles per hour. Heavy rain, hail and dangerous lightening should be expected. Take all necessary precautions or head to the nearest port. This is the United States Coast Guard Moriches Group out". Another scenario might be: "Securitay, Securitay, Securitay this is SeaTow Freeport approaching the Loop Parkway Bridge with a 30 foot powerboat in stern tow. We will be transiting the middle section, southbound with limited control. Please give a clear passage and no wake. We will be standing by on channel 16. This is SeaTow Freeport out".

A second-priority message is one that concerns the safety of the vessel or persons on board. That is to say that you are in need of assistance from other vessels but the situation is not life threatening at this time. You just want to make others aware of your situation in case it worsens. These messages are preceded with the words Pan-Pan (spoken three times). This indicates the urgency of the message and takes priority over all other transmissions, except for a Mayday. An example of this is: "Pan-Pan, Pan-Pan, Pan-Pan, All Stations. This is the motor vessel LynnAnn, LynnAnn, LynnAnn. We are taking on water after a collision with a submerged log. Our pumps are keeping up with the flow of water at this time. We are a twenty five foot white cabin cruiser with blue trim and have two children and two adults on board. We are one mile south of the Fire Island Inlet and are adrift. This is the LynnAnn, Over". At this time you would await a response and typically the Coast Guard will arrange to speak with you every fifteen minutes until the situation is controlled or you require assistance. After the Pan-Pan emergency is over you need to cancel the message. This would sound like: "Pan-Pan, Pan-Pan, Hello all stations, Hello all stations. This is the LynnAnn the time is 10:00 AM. Cancel Pan-Pan. Over". Sometimes, instead of the words cancel Pan-Pan, you may hear Seelonce Feenee. This is french for silence finished. At this time normal radio transmissions are continued. Another example of a second priority message is "Pan-Pan, Pan-Pan, Pan-Pan, Hello all stations. Hello all stations. This is the United States Coast Guard Baltimore Group with an Urgent Marine Information Broadcast (UMIB). At 13:30 the Coast Guard received a distress call on VHFM channel 16 with no position or nature of the distress reported. All mariners are asked to keep a sharp lookout, assist if possible and notify the Coast Guard of any sightings. This is the United States Coast Guard Baltimore Group out".

A first-priority message is one that concerns a grave and imminent danger which is a threat to life or property and immediate assistance is needed. These messages are preceded with the word Mayday, spoken three times. This indicates the extremely serious nature of the distress and takes priority over all other transmissions. Mayday comes from the french word M'aidez, meaning help me. An example of a first priority message is: "Mayday, Mayday, Mayday, This is the motor vessel LynnAnn, LynnAnn, LynnAnn. Our position is 39 degrees 04.94 minutes North, 74 degrees 58.43 minutes west. We have a 65 year old male onboard who is in cardiac arrest. CPR is being administered. We require medical assistance at once. The LynnAnn is a 42 foot white sport fisherman with blue trim. I will be standing by on channel 16. This is the LynnAnn, Over". Now you just wait for a return response and hopefully a Medevac, or evacuation of the victim from the vessel by helicopter. After the distress is over or the imposed silence to other radio traffic is over, you may again hear a transmission that cancels the Mayday or the words Seelonce Feenee.

Your responsibility is to stand by during either a Mayday or Pan-Pan and make sure the Coast Guard has responded. You may be in a position to assist by relaying a message if there is a problem with reception or you may be close enough to render assistance by going to the vessel in distress. The Coast Guard will advise and ask for assistance if it is needed. If the Coast Guard does not respond, then you should respond and do whatever is appropriate. This will include trying to contact the Coast Guard on behalf of the vessel in distress.

You need to be aware of these special situations which may arise, but the more mundane use of the radio is what you will most commonly encounter. Hailing or trying to contact another vessel is a valuable use of your radio. Quite simply, you start on channel 16 or 9 and you wait for a break in other transmissions. Key the mike (press the push to talk button) and speak clearly holding the microphone 2-3 inches from your mouth.

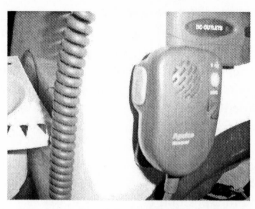

Your transmission should sound something like this: "Obsession, Obsession. This is the LynnAnn. Over". If Obsession hears you they will respond by saying: "LynnAnn this is Obsession. Your response now is: Obsession, switch to six-eight. Over". You then change to channel 68 and start by saying: "Obsession, this is the LynnAnn" and your conversation goes from there. If you did not hear a response on channel 16, you may try again in 2 minutes. After three consecutive attempts you must wait 15 minutes before trying again. Also, it is against regulations to have any non emergency conversation on channel 16. Just call, make contact and move to another channel. Turn on your radio on a beautiful Sunday in August and you will see why these rules are necessary.

If you want to check out your radio equipment you may ask for a radio check. This must not be done on channel 16. You may do it on channel 9 or another working channel, one that has no specially assigned use. The best way to do it is to predetermine a time with a friend and hail him on channel 9 preferably. Do it according to regulations and switch to another channel. This allows both of you to test your equipment and hone your skills with the use of the radio. In case of a failure of your primary radio or antenna you may want to consider carrying a backup. There are several inexpensive hand held radios on the market that fit the bill perfectly. I look for two important features when buying one. Most have all the necessary things like weather channels and scanning capabilities, but you also need an extra power source. Some operate on disposable as well as rechargeable batteries. Rechargeable batteries usually require AC power to charge them. If you pick it up and its dead, you can use disposable batteries which you should always carry with you. Some radios can be plugged into a cigarette lighter which every boat should have. This however assumes that the boats battery is operable at this time. A true spare radio should operate independently of the boat, its battery or antenna.

Many people feel that because they carry a cellular phone they do not need a VHF radio in the first place and definitely not a spare. Cell phones on board are great. They free up the already congested radio and offer private conversations. That is fine if you want your conversation private. When in distress pick up the VHF mike not the cell phone. The Coast Guard has set up a special number *CG or *24 to contact them, but definitely discourages their use in an emergency. You want as many people as possible to know that you are in trouble. This will facilitate the arrival of assistance. Remember, you want to get the message out to as many people as possible. The other problem with cell phones is that their signal is not traceable. What I mean, is that with a VHF radio the Coast Guard can employ the use of a radio direction finder. This can allow your rescuers to home in on your location. The Coast Guard may even ask you for a long count. This means that you key the mike and count slowly from one to ten. This gives them time to get a fix on your location. With a cell phone this is not possible. If your VHF fails, by all means use your cell phone. Just do not count on it as your first or only line of defense. Interestingly, the Coast Guard reports that 10% of all Mayday calls come in by cell phone.

To recap, do not hesitate to use your radio as long as you use it properly and for the right reasons. Be aware of its other uses such as Securitay, Pan-Pan, and Mayday. Most boat supply stores have preprinted instructions outlining the parameters for these types of transmissions. You should plan ahead by filling one of them out and leaving it onboard in a dry area. In an emergency you or someone else can read it over the radio without having to think about the details. Also, make a note of the working stations available to you in your area so you have it planned out ahead of time. Listening to the radio regularly when on board is a great way to learn its proper use. You can listen to what others do and try to see what they do right and what they do wrong. Its also safer to keep it on as you can keep abreast of the weather and any other potential hazards. Many radios have a NOAA weather alert function that gives an audible signal whenever an urgent weather message is being broadcast. You may also find yourself in a position to help someone else. That is really what its all about, keeping safe and helping others keep safe. When you have the opportunity to help someone out on the water, you will find you feel great for days. However small your aid is, it is very rewarding.

Returning now to the Coast Guard requirements, the next item, Visual Distress Signals, can be very confusing. To simplify things, you are required to carry visual distress signals which are Coast Guard approved and have not expired. For boats over 16 feet you need to fulfill both a daytime and nighttime requirement even if you do not use your boat at night. If your boat is under 16 feet you need to only fulfill the nighttime requirement. To fulfill the nighttime requirement, only pyrotechnic devices are Coast Guard approved. Pyrotechnic devices for night use include handheld red flares, red aerial flares and red parachute flares. A minimum of three of these devices in any combination are required. Pyrotechnic devices for daytime use are handheld or aerial red flares which are marked, "Approved for Day Use" and floating or handheld orange smoke devices. A minimum of three of these devices in any combination are required. The non-pyrotechnic device also approved for daytime use is a three foot square, orange flag. To further clarify, you need three devices for night use and three devices for day use, totaling six. Or you may carry three devices approved for both day and night use. For example, you may carry three handheld red flares with proper approval for both situations. In the dark, these inexpensive devices are very visible. In the daytime, however I do not feel they are visible enough.

Depending upon your background, level of confidence and the distance you travel offshore, you may want to upgrade to aerial flares. Keep in mind that these devices are basically firearms. They require a certain level of expertise to use properly and safely. They have quite a bit of recoil when they launch. While they can be seen from a greater distance than handheld flares, if you do not feel confident in your ability to handle them safely, then do not have them on board. The last thing that you want to do is to make a bad situation worse by injuring yourself or someone else with such a device.

My feelings on the subject are that you should carry several handheld flares for night use. I carry at least six. For day use, I carry several orange smoke signals and an orange flag. I carry the flag just because it's inexpensive, takes up relatively no space and is always there if you need it. I do not rely solely on combined day/night flares because in the places I boat, I do not feel they will provide enough noticeable exposure during the day. Often, I use my small skiff to run way up into the salt marshes to get clams and oysters. If I break down or get injured in one of those locations; I am almost invisible. Orange smoke can change all that. It will rise well above my position and is an unmistakable signal. Handheld flares or an orange flag, do not make me feel safe enough in that situation. Even if I use my VHF radio to call someone for assistance, I can still use the smoke to guide them to me once they get close. I also carry aerial flares, which I can use in the same situation. I make sure to familiarize myself with their use in the spring and fall when I check out all my equipment. I commonly boat in remote locations and in the dead of winter when there are not many other people around, I like the idea of the extra visibility these provide. They alert people to the fact that I am in trouble. I then would resort to my hand held devices to guide them to my position. You may notice flares marked SOLAS (Safety of Life at Sea) in the stores. They are a brighter flare that exceeds Coast Guard standards. In turn, they are more expensive. You must assess your risk by thinking of the location and distance offshore that you travel. As usual, do what you think is right for your particular situation. Base your choice on what you feel you need. A brighter flare has its obvious advantages, but of course, there is always a trade off. All flares burn hot and give off slag which can burn you or your boat. SOLAS flares do burn very hot and may be somewhat difficult to hold. Set price aside while you make your choice and do what feel comfortable with.

I keep all of these devices together in a bright orange dry box marked Safety Equipment. I throw in a signaling mirror, whistle and any other gear that I feel may be necessary in a pinch. All pyrotechnic devices have expiration dates on them.

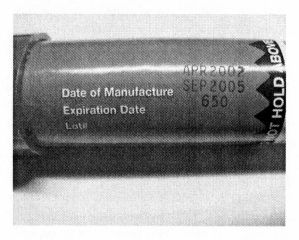

They are approved for a total of 42 months. Check the dates twice a year and replace them as necessary. They do have chemicals in them that degrade over time. These chemicals affect the intensity of the device as well as their ability to ignite, so there is a rational reason behind it. I still keep some expired flares on board as spares, but make sure to get rid of the aging ones. It is advisable to not set off flares older than say five years, as they may misfire and cause an injury. Flares are classified as hazardous waste and must not be disposed of in the regular garbage. Look for collection programs run by Boat/US, the Coast Guard or ask your sanitation department if they will take them for you. Definitely do not discard them by setting them off.

Several companies make cost effective kits that have everything you need packaged in a neat case. These work out well and make meeting your requirements easy. Some companies will even send you a reminder when your flares are near expiration. I usually buy these products locally because, if you order by mail, hazardous shipping charges will apply, making these more expensive than they need to be.

If you are out on the water and see a distress signal you should first notify the Coast Guard. You do this via your VHF radio. You would hail them on channel 16 by saying, "Coast Guard, Coast Guard this is the Lynn Ann". The Coast Guard should respond by saying, "Lynn Ann, this is Coast Guard Station Jones Beach". You will then tell them that you have just seen a red aerial flare in the Haunts Creek area. They may ask you several more questions and then ask you to stand by in case your needed and to keep a lookout for additional signals. The Coast Guard may try to hail this vessel or they may ask you to try. Keep in mind that if they are using visual distress signals, they probably do not have a radio or it is inoperable.

Remember, your first line of defense in an emergency is to let someone else know that you are having a problem and are in distress. If your radio fails to operate, remember your backup hand held radio. Assuming that this also fails to make contact, your next option is to use your flares or smoke. You have a limited number of these devices so you have to make each one count. Try to wait until you see another boat. If you cannot wait or do not see anyone for a while, use one anyway. You never know who may be around. Make noise with your whistle and use your signaling mirror. Put your orange flag out as high as possible. Wave your arms over your head, make noise with your horn and try anything you can think of to attract attention to yourself. Keep your head about you and deal with the situation as best and as safely as possible.

Realizing that visual distress signals, when seen by someone, will usually start a search and rescue. You should never use one to practice or play with. I was once in a waterfront campground on the Chesapeake Bay and there was a group of vacationing police officers on several bay front sites. They were using expired road flares to start their campfires at night. They get very hot and start fires quickly. There is a lesson to be learned from that alone. Well, someone from the opposite shore or on a boat must have seen a red flare and called the Coast Guard. They sent out a boat to investigate. No one on shore put two and two together until we saw them again the next night. They handled things tactfully by having the campground send around a notice explaining what was happening and requesting that it stop. Which it did.

The same goes for your VHF. What some people may think of as a joke can start a process which can cost a lot of money and put peoples lives at risk. The Coast Guard is required to investigate every distress call even if they feel it is a hoax. When they begin a search and rescue, people are put at risk. Additionally, resources are tied up which may be needed elsewhere for a legitimate distress call. Teach your children the proper use of the radio and what the consequences are for improper use of the radio. The Coast Guard refers hoax distress cases to the United States

Attorney's Office for prosecution. Knowingly and willfully transmitting a hoax distress call is felony. It is punishable by up to six years in prison, a $250,000.00 fine and restitution to the Coast Guard for all costs involved in responding to the distress. These costs can be quite hefty. It costs about $6500.00 an hour for a rescue helicopter on down to $2000.00 an hour for a patrol boat. The maximum civil penalty is $5000.00 Remember, the parent is responsible for the child's actions in these cases. Sadly enough, it is not always the child that causes the trouble. Realize what can happen.

To further drive the point home, the Coast Guard estimates that in 2002 it spent $18 million nationally in wasted aircraft and boat searches. With the number of hoax calls received increasing every year, the Coast Guard has gone high tech to help combat the problem. Through the use of sophisticated equipment to record a Visual Voice Signature from the hoax caller, the electronic signature from their VHF radio and new Radio Direction Finders on land and at sea, agents are really cracking down.

Back in March of 1990 the hoax distress call issue was brought to the forefront by the Sol e Mar incident. The Sol e Mar was a fishing boat operating in the waters off of Martha's Vineyard, Massachusetts. The Coast Guard operator on duty received a distress call believed to be from the Sol e Mar, which was reportedly sinking. The Coast Guard was unable to contact the vessel in distress. Within minutes, another call was received from a prank caller who was laughing. At the time, the Coast Guard erroneously believed that the two calls were from the same source and no search was initiated. Several days later the Sol e Mar was reported overdue and a search was begun at that time. The vessel and crew were never found.

The problem is not just children doing the wrong thing. It is estimated that 30 percent of hoax calls come from children, 27 percent from teens and 33 percent from adults.

That's right, a full third of this problem is from adults. Do your part. If you have information pertaining to a hoax, call the Coast Guard's hotline to help out. The number is 1-800-2NO-HOAX.

The rest of the necessary safety requirements can be lumped together into one section. Boats less than 39' in length must carry an efficient sound producing device. You should have a couple plastic whistles. Put one on your key ring and another in your orange safety box. All boats should also have a horn. Believe it or not, it is not always standard equipment. Either install one or buy one that operates with compressed air. They have some which are rechargeable by the use of a small hand pump. That way they are always ready when you need one. Boats over 39 feet also need to have a bell on board to use when visibility is restricted.

On boats with enclosed spaces, The Coast Guard requires that all engine compartments and enclosed areas which house fuel tanks have proper ventilation. Also, engine compartments with gasoline engines with electric cranking motors (just about every large gasoline engine in existence) require the use of power operated exhaust blowers, operated from the instrument panel. This requirement should be taken care of by the manufacturer of the boat. If you have any questions you should contact a marine surveyor to evaluate your particular situation. Also required on all gas powered engines with carburetors (except outboards) are backfire flame arrestors. These prevent open flames in the engine compartment if the engine backfires. This is necessary for obvious reasons.

The final Coast Guard requirement is navigation lights which must be displayed during sunset to sunrise. Again, this should be taken care of by the manufacturer. Your responsibility is to make sure they are in working order and that you have them turned on at night or during the day when there is restricted visibility.

While not a Coast Guard requirement, prudent boaters need

to be aware of ways to control an influx of water. Water can enter your boat in a number of ways. It can be from large waves breaking over the bow, often referred to as boarding waves, or perhaps a steady rainfall for several days which can cause quite an accumulation. Water can enter below the waterline from damaged running gear, a broken or ruptured through hull fitting or even a defect in the hull. In the case of inboard powered boats, an improperly adjusted or worn stuffing box can be the culprit. The stuffing box or gland as it may be called is a device which controls water intrusion around the propeller shaft. When properly packed and adjusted, a slow trickle of water is normal. Even this slow trickle, over time needs to be evacuated. This is the job of the bilge pump or pumps.

The bilge pump is an electrically powered motor which is operated by a float switch. A float switch is just that. It has a buoyant lever and when the water level is high enough, the lever rises and activates the pump. As the water level drops, the switch lever falls and the pump shuts down. For proper and reliable operation, this switch requires that the bilge be kept clean at all times. Debris can accumulate, and prevent the lever from operating properly. It can keep the pump in the on position, draining the battery or burning out the pump. This will render the pump useless and leave the boat unprotected. Covers are available for these switches to protect them, as are various automatic pumps which have the ability to turn on at set intervals and stay on as long as they detect water moving past the impeller.

Most boat manufacturers wire the bilge pump directly from the battery to a three way switch. These switches have positions for automatic or manual operation, as well as for an off position. The switch is best left in the automatic position at all times. Manual operation is a nice option to have if the float switch fails or you want to pump out water at other times or more completely than the float switch will allow. Keep in mind that any mechanical device can fail. Frequent checking of your boat is necessary to avoid problems. It is often reported that a major cause of sinking is the failure of the owner to check the boat regularly. One of the first things you need to do when you arrive at your boat is to check the water level in the bilge. Know what a normal amount of water is, and visually check that the pump and switch are in good condition.

The bilge pump itself is rated by flow capacity in gallons per hour (gph). These ratings are under ideal circumstances which do not exist in the real world. Specifically, they are based on having a full 12 volts of power and no head. Head is defined as the resistance the pump has to work against before it can evacuate water. It encompasses both the height that the pump needs to raise the water, known as the static head. As well as any resistance from the type and diameter of hose used, the diameter of the thru hull fitting and a multitude of other factors. This resistance is known as frictional head. We need to know this only so far as to realize that we will not see performance close to the gph rating on the pump. Generally, when choosing a new pump, it is prudent to get the largest capacity pump that will fit the space you are putting it in. If the space is very large, getting a pump that is one or two times larger than what you are replacing should be enough to overcome any resistance your system has.

In case of total bilge pump failure, a plastic bailer or even half of a plastic bottle can save the day. Even better than that is a manual hand pump. They are cheap, small and evacuate a lot of water very efficiently. To help reduce the flow of unwanted water, I also carry a package of wooden plugs which can be pushed through a damaged thru hull fitting, broken hose or valve. Just push them in the hole or hose to stop the flow of water enough so that your bilge pump can keep up with it. They come several to a package for under ten dollars and are good insurance. It is a good idea to tie one onto each thru hull fitting so that it is readily available if needed. Remember, if you are maneuvering around in your engine compartment, never step on a thru hull fitting. You never know just how strong the hull is at that point. The entire fitting can be pushed right through the hull, resulting in a horrible situation. I also like to keep some rags around which can also be stuffed into a leak to slow it down a bit. I always have several rolls of electrical tape handy. I feel it holds better than duct tape in a wet environment. Everyone has their favorite material. I have a friend that swears by Potty Wax. That's right, the same stuff that you use to prevent leaks under your toilet. It is waterproof, sticky and can easily be stuffed into holes, pipes, etc. It is also cheap. A box of Marine Tex is also a must have onboard. It is a two part epoxy that sticks to just about everything. Its most important quality is that it sets up under water. It is a great quick fix which can save your day or even more.

A few other items should also be stowed onboard just in case they become necessary. A First Aid Kit is a valuable item. You can purchase pre packaged kits from the drug store and they are fine. Personally, I like a bit more than they offer. I use a medium sized Rubbermaid container that I fill with my personal favorites. They include each child's favorite band aides, adhesive tape, gauze pads, Betadine, triple antibiotic ointment, Dermaplast Spray, an ace bandage, mosquito and tick repellant, aspirin or your favorite pain reliever, sun screen, cold packs, tweezers, Q tips, sting relief swabs and a dozen other items that

I like to have around. Everyone has their favorite remedy for this or that. Pick it up and put it in.

A new product which can save the day if you have it onboard is called Prop Aid. It temporarily corrects for a spun prop, allowing you to get home. A spun prop occurs when the propeller of an outboard or stern drive hits the bottom or an object, very hard. The plastic prop hub spins, preventing damage to the prop and lower unit. It is evident when the boat cannot accelerate because as torque increases, the prop spins freely on the hub and cannot push the boat along. While it helps prevent damage, it can leave you stranded. This new product corrects this temporarily by replacing the prop's existing retaining washer with Prop Aid. This does however require that you have a prop wrench onboard and can safely do the job.

By far however, the single most important item to have on board is a good flashlight. You cannot fix the problem if you cannot see enough to diagnose the problem. Being able to see is half of the battle. Not far behind in importance is a good knife. A lock back is necessary so the blade will not try to close on your fingers. I personally like a knife that I can open using one hand only. Store your knife in a safe location, like in your emergency dry box. Make sure any children know that this box is off limits. Use the knife with discretion. Close it after each time you use it and never use it in rough seas unless absolutely necessary. I know several people that will not board a boat or even be on a dock for that matter, without a knife. Most also feel that the best place for it is strapped to your waist. In that location, it is always accessible by you and you never have to fish around for it in the bottom of your pocket or any other location. Do what you feel comfortable with.

Chapter 3

GETTING OUT

*Your success depends mainly upon
what you think of yourself and
whether you believe in yourself.*
—*William J. H. Boetcker*

Finally, finally, finally we can get out on the water and enjoy ourselves. We can find confidence in the fact that we have a good working knowledge of boats and we have an arsenal of safety equipment on board. Better than that, we have the know how to use it timely and properly. So lets go. Well, not quite yet. I know your dying to get out, but just a few more things.

Before you leave home you need to make sure that you tell someone, who will be remaining on land, where you are going and when you plan to return. This is called a Float Plan. For a short trip this could be as simple as calling a friend or family member and telling them that you are going fishing in Haunts Creek and south of Meadow Island. You plan to return no later than 4:00 PM and will call to let him know that you are back. You need to be diligent in making this phone call when you return or calling this person if you have a change of plans. They also need to know what to do, if you are not back on time. They should first call you at home, on your cell phone or beep you. If possible, they should go to the marina to see if your boat is back in your slip. If they cannot go to the marina, they should call the marina and have them check your slip. If they still cannot find you, the Float Plan should provide them with the phone number of the nearest Coast Guard Station. They should call the Coast Guard and notify them that you are overdue. Give them the name and description of the vessel. The number of people onboard and the area that you planned to be in. Also, tell them that you have a VHF radio and routinely monitor channel 16. This person's responsibilities are now complete and the Coast Guard will take over. If you hear from the missing vessel you should notify the Coast Guard right away. The Coast Guard will not automatically initiate a search. They will first put out an Urgent Marine Information Broadcast (UMIB) on VHF channel 16. At their discretion, they may or may not begin to search later.

If you are planning a longer trip, you should prepare a written Float Plan. This should include an overview of your plans, destinations, estimated time of arrival at each location and expected return date and time. You should arrange a phone in schedule to keep someone on shore aware of any problems, delays or plan changes you are encountering. Include in this packet any information that may help the Coast Guard locate you such as fuel capacity, navigation equipment onboard, as well as a good written description of your vessel. Again, leave this with a reliable person onshore. Float Plans can not be filed directly with the Coast Guard as they do not have the manpower to deal with them.

Sample Float Plan

Name of Person Filing Float Plan and Telephone Numbers

Description of Boat: Type _____ Color _____ Trim _____ Registration # _____
Length _____ Name _____ Make _____ Other Pertinent Info _____

Number of Persons Onboard _____
Name, Age, Address, Telephone #

_____

_____

_____

Engine Type and Number _____ H.P. _____ Fuel Capacity _____

Survival Equipment: PFD's _____ Flares _____ Smoke Signals _____ VHF _____
Raft _____ Food _____ Other _____

Trip Expectations: Departure Time _____ From _____ Going To _____
Expected Time and Day of Return _____ No Later Than _____
Other Pertinent Itinerary Info _____

Automobile Licence Plate # _____ Type and Color _____ Trailer Plate # _____
Where Parked _____

If Not Returned By _____ (Time and Date) Call the Coast Guard or
Local Authorities at: _____

_____

Other Pertinent Information: _____

Now you are ready to head to the marina or launching ramp. Upon arrival check the general appearance of your boat. Is the boat listing to one side or sitting low in the water? This could indicate a lot of water is in the bilge and possibly a failed pump. I open up any hatches, doors and if applicable, the engine compartment. A visual check is a must. Look for things like an oil or gas sheen in the bilge water or surrounding water. Most importantly, smell for anything unusual such as fuel. Your nose is a great detector of fuel vapor, but it is a good idea to install a fume detector. This is an electronic device which can save your life and boat. Some units can detect fumes from sources other than just gasoline. These include cooking fuels, solvents and cleaning products. Some of the higher end detectors will even automatically turn on your bilge blower.

One very serious problem, that these detectors cannot help with, is Carbon Monoxide (CO) contamination. A separate CO detector is a must for any boat with enclosed spaces. CO can make you sick very quickly and in high concentrations can prove fatal in just a few minutes. The most important thing to know is that the symptoms of exposure to CO are drowsiness, headache, dizziness and loss of coordination. They are basically the same symptoms people experience if they are sea sick. Keep this in mind if you or your passengers feel sick. A CO detector removes the guesswork. If it sounds, shut down all sources of CO such as your engine or generator. Open all hatches and windows to ventilate the enclosed spaces as much as possible and get all people up on deck into the fresh air. CO can enter your boat in many, many ways, most commonly through leaks in the exhaust system. Also, back drafting can occur, where exhaust is pulled into the boat's cabin due to a void of air formed behind the cabin as the boat moves ahead. This is known as the Station Wagon effect. Buy a good detector and perform any necessary maintenance to keep it functioning properly. When a CO detector sounds, never be fooled into thinking that it is a malfunction. Always assume that there is an abundance of CO. The better units do not malfunction often. Get into the fresh air immediately so you can evaluate the situation before any more exposure can occur.

When I am satisfied that the boat is in the same condition that I left it in, I begin to load my gear and passengers. If any children or non-swimmers are with us, they don their PFD's in the parking lot before venturing out onto the dock. Once everything is stowed in its proper place, it is time to prepare for departure. If there is a battery switch, I turn it from off to the starting battery. It is customary in dual battery setups to use only one battery to start, unless you have a particularly hard start; then you can choose to use both batteries in parallel. The proper use of a battery selector switch will always leave one fully charged battery in case one gets accidentally drained from over use. Make sure you have a feature called alternator disconnect which will protect the engines alternator if the switch is mistakenly switched to the off position while the engine is running. Keep in mind that while running, to charge both batteries you must set the switch to the "both" position. This is important, as you need to keep both batteries fully charged at all times.

If so equipped, I turn on the bilge blower. The bilge blower is a standard bit of equipment on inboard powered boats. It exhausts out any fuel vapors which may have accumulated in the bilge or engine compartment. This could present an explosion hazard when you turn the key to start the engine as there may be open sparks present. This should run long enough to completely exchange the air at least once. This should take at least five minutes, maybe longer depending upon the size of the boat. During this time, I mount and turn on my electronics and make sure they are working properly. I also turn on my VHF radio and select the weather channel to listen for any changes in the forecast which may affect us.

If you have an outboard or stern drive, now is the time to lower the engine or outdrive into the water and visually confirm that its where you want it. Next, start your engine according to the manufacturers recommendations. If you have twin engines, start them one at a time. Whatever type of engine you have, it is the first few minutes after a cold start that the majority of the wear and tear on the engine occurs. When the engine is initially cranked and started, lubrication is at a minimum until the engine reaches operating temperature. You should allow your engine to warm up at idle. That is to say, do not leave too soon. Also, check to see that you are discharging coolant water. Remember that telltale stream of water we spoke about in Chapter 1. For inboards you will see this water discharged through the exhaust system.

Once the engine is warmed up and you are satisfied that all your systems are operating properly, it is time to go. Give your passengers instructions as to what to do, even if its just where to sit. Make sure everyone knows to keep their hands in. If you do want someone to fend off pilings or other boats, give them a boat hook to use. Do not allow them to do this with their hands. It is a very easy way to get hurt. Check the wind and current to determine if it will help or hurt your departure. Cast off your lines and either bring them onboard or leave them on the dock. Do not let them drop into the water. Invariably, they will find your propeller on its way past. I look around to see that my path is clear and that no other boats are leaving their slip at the same time. I like to get moving by bumping the throttle. That is, I nudge it forward into gear just until it engages and then drop it back into neutral. The boat begins to move slowly and the influences of wind and current begin to show themselves. You now can either counter them or take advantage of them as their effects become apparent. Move the steering wheel accordingly and bump again. Reposition the wheel and bump again. This slow movement allows you time to react to the many other factors that affect your boat. Soon you will be out of your slip and moving out. If your speed becomes to great in these usually confined locations, do not be afraid to go into neutral. Your boat has a minimum speed in forward and often this is too fast. Neutral will slow you down and give you more control. As long as the boat is making way, that is moving ahead, you will have steering ability. If you begin to lose control bump the throttle again.

If things do not go smoothly, your initial reaction will be to hit the throttle to get out of the situation that you are in.

This instinct comes from driving an automobile, as well as from the insecurity we feel because we do not have the ability to brake. We have the need to do something. On the water you must resist that urge at all costs. Your boat is affected by many factors that your car is not, and basically, your boat just does not work like a car. It tends to respond poorly to abrupt and fast actions. Your car turns by positioning the front tires and moving the vehicle. Your boat turns by positioning the engine or rudder in the rear of the vessel and moving. In very simple terms, your boat turns in forward the way your car turns in reverse. The actions of the two, even when in the same direction, forward or reverse, are entirely different from one another and cannot be compared, especially because current and wind usually have no effect on your car.

In a bad situation, such as getting too close to other boats in a marina, go against your instincts. In most situations this means slowing down, act by positioning the wheel and bumping the throttle. Then let the boat react. Act and react, use forward and reverse until you are out of the jam. I do not care what the size of your boat is or what means of propulsion you have, this is the way to turn a situation around and into your favor. Do not lose your cool and do not go fast. I think one of the most commonly asked question for a new boater is: "What is the best way for me to get out of my slip?" Really, there is never one best way. We are dealing with an ever changing, dynamic situation. The answer has to do with what works that particular day. The common theme is slow speed, constant control and proper evaluation of variables like wind and current.

Before we can get very far, we need to stop for fuel. Ideally, this chore should be taken care of without a lot of passengers onboard. It is safer that way and a lot less confusing. Make sure that you purchase your fuel from a reputable location. I prefer to stick with a name brand station for no other reason than if you get stuck with bad fuel you know who to complain to. The biggest problem with fuel is usually water contamination. When I am boating out of my usual territory, this is a factor that is usually out of my control. To tip the scales in my favor when away from home, my personal preference is to go to the busiest place I can. If I see a lot of people buying gas they all cannot be wrong.

I prefer to approach the dock against the current, as this gives me more control. You may need to motor past once to see which way the current is moving. As always, I come in slowly and as close to parallel to the dock that I can. At my desired location I give a gentle burst of reverse to stop my forward momentum and I am done. In a single screw boat, if I must pull in between two boats, I again will come in slowly against the current. I nudge the bow in to my desired location and have either the dock personnel or someone on my boat tie off the bow. I have them do this rather snugly. I do not want a lot of play. Then, I turn the wheel hard away from the dock and apply light forward throttle. This pivots me off of the bow line and brings my stern in smartly to the dock.

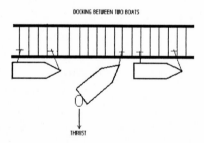

DOCKING BETWEEN TWO BOATS

THRUST

In a vessel with twin screws, this can be done in one fluid motion by using your throttles to steer the boat into the desired location.

Tie off and shut everything down. Make sure the key is all the way to the off position. I hope I do not need to tell you not to smoke. Close off all hatches, doors and windows to prevent fumes from settling below. If you need to mix oil with your fuel, put it in before fueling so it will mix well. If you have portable tanks, detach them and fill them on the dock. If the tanks are too large or permanently installed, then bring the hose to them and begin filling. Make sure, whatever type of tanks you have, that the metal fill nozzle is in contact with the rim of the tank. This prevents a buildup of static electricity. Make sure that you do not overfill the tanks. You need to leave room for expansion and you also do not want to spill any overboard. This can be done accidentally through your tank's vent. Know your tank's capacity, monitor the amount going in and be careful. There is an inexpensive little device that suction cups over your boats vent opening while fueling to catch any fuel that would otherwise end up in the water. When we think of an oil or fuel spill, we generally think of large tankers such as the Exxon Valdez. The fact of the matter is that the cumulative effect of small spills is much greater and more damaging to our environment. The Oil pollution act of 1990 addresses this problem directly. It defines a spill as any fuel or oil that creates a sheen on the water. We all know that this can be a very small amount. A single quart of oil creates a sheen that can cover two acres of water. If you are fueling and a small spill occurs, you are responsible to stop the flow of fuel and therefore prevent the spill from getting worse. You must then initiate a cleanup and report the spill to the Coast Guard or the National Response Center at 1-800-424-8802. Fault is not an issue; the spill is. Just for causing the spill you may be fined between $50 and $500. The faster it is reported and the more you do to contain it and clean it up, the better your case will be. Failure to report the spill carries a much stiffer penalty which is criminal in nature and can be up to $250,000. Insurance will not cover fines and penalties. Boat owners are legally responsible for up to $500,000 in containment, cleanup and environmental damage costs. This applies even if you have done nothing wrong. You should check with your insurance carrier to see if your policy has fuel spill coverage. Boat/US has $500,000 in fuel spill coverage standard on all its policies. The best part is that they have a 24 hour dispatch service to facilitate the clean up. The Coast Guard looks favorably upon people who act quickly. This makes it easy. Most towing services, such as TowBoat/US, are certified oil spill responders. If all else fails, call them directly.

To help in the cleanup, absorbent cloths should be kept on board. They are placed on top of the spill and removed when saturated. Booms, which can be used to contain a spill are desirable and may be available at some fuel docks. They are not however the kind of thing you should be expected to have yourself. Use of a dispersant, such as dishwashing soap to make the sheen disappear is also illegal and punishable by fines up to $27,500. Dispersants make the fuel or oil form into droplets which then sink and do greater harm to the environment.

When at the fuel dock use a vent cover and never top off the tank. It is better to stop short of a full tank then to let fuel spill into the water. Fines and penalties are one thing. Our impact on the environment is another. Pay attention to what you are doing and all will be well.

After fueling, close the gas cap tightly, wipe up any spillage and discard the rag properly on the dock. Usually the attendant will take care of it for you. Reopen all hatches, doors and windows. Smell for any leaked fuel and look around for a sheen in the bilge water. Turn on your bilge blower if you have one and let it run for the specified time, usually four or five minutes. After settling up with the attendant your ready to go. The gas dock is potentially the most dangerous place around, so get going as soon as you are convinced all is in order.

One more thing worth mentioning is that you should carry a spare gas cap. The thin chain that keeps the cap attached to the tank is subject to breakage and I have yet to see a gas cap that floats. You cannot operate your boat without a cap, as fuel will spill and water is sure to get into the tank. A spare cap can save the day and your engine(s). They are available from your manufacturer or the boat supply store, but almost never from the fuel dock.

You can pull off the dock the same way you arrived. If the coast is clear ahead, pull off gradually and slowly, avoiding any sharp turns until you are sure your stern has cleared the pilings. You can also pivot off the bow line. Turn your wheel hard toward the dock and give a little bit of forward throttle. The stern kicks away from the dock. Release the bow line and gently back away. On a twin screw vessel you have many more options, such as walking the boat off the dock laterally. Practice makes perfect. I cannot give you all of the possible scenarios you will encounter nor discuss all of the types of boat configurations and their particular qualities. What I have tried to do is provide you with some insight into one man's technique. You invariably will master your own technique if you get out there and confidently do it again and again.

Chapter 4

GETTING THERE

There's some end at last for the man
who follows a path; mere rambling
is interminable.

—Marcus Annaeus Seneca

Once out of the confines of the marina you can begin to relax and have fun. Here is where a bit of preplanning will allow you to really enjoy the water. If you are boating in your home territory and going to your usual places, just follow the channels staying well within the buoys or markers that you usually use to guide you. Be mindful of the basics, Red, Right, Return. You keep the red, even numbered buoys or markers to your right or starboard side when returning from seaward. Since we are not returning, but heading out, we keep the green, odd numbered buoys to starboard.

The green buoys are called cans and are cylindrically shaped. The red buoys are called nuns and are cone shaped. This is important to remember, because at night or during other times of decreased visibility, the colors may not be apparent. The shapes however, should always be discernable. To stay within the channel, draw an imaginary line between the greens and between the reds and this will mark the channel boundaries. Stay within these imaginary lines and on the starboard side of the channel.

Additionally, a buoy that is both green and red is called a mid-channel buoy and often marks a bifurcation or a merging of two channels.

In some areas Range Markers are used to easily guide you down the center of a channel. You just line up the patterns on two markers and you are home free.

Remember also that when markers are placed on poles, the same rules as buoys apply for color, numbering and shape.

You absolutely need to have good charts onboard of your boating area.

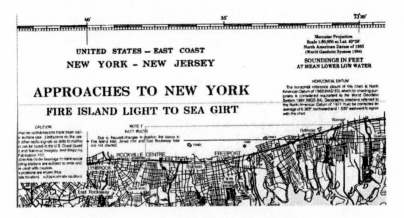

Remember, nautical charts are never referred to as maps. These need to be in a scale or size which gives you good detail of the area. Most general use charts are about 1:80,000. Remember, a 1:100,000 chart is a smaller scale chart, which will offer less detail than a 1:80,000 chart. In your home waters, these are for reference and should be looked at from time to time to refresh your memory. When venturing out into new or less familiar territories, you should really study them. Some people prefer chart booklets such as those put out by Chart Kit Booklets. They are easier to handle on a small boat, especially in the wind. Keep in mind however, that the charts you buy in the store are basically out of date when you get them. Some are actually very old and have not been updated in years. This of course is a problem. For example, located about 7 miles from Sandy Hook, NJ was Ambrose Light Tower, a 136 foot tall structure adorned with lights which are visible for 25 miles. It marks the entrance to one of the busiest ports in the world, New York Harbor. On October 5, 1996 it was damaged beyond repair by the AEGEO, a 754 foot Liberian registered oil tanker carrying 18 million gallons of oil to Woodbridge, NJ. At about 4:25 AM the tanker somehow collided with the tower and destroyed one of its legs. The damage was so severe the entire tower had to be dismantled. The Coast Guard put out a new more modern replacement, but they put it a mile and a half away from the old one. Unless you realize this and update its new position on your chart, then your chart is wrong.

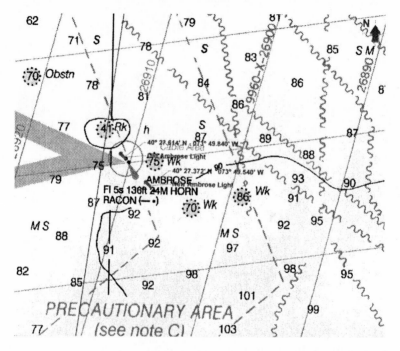

Think about these huge ships which use Ambrose every day as they approach New York Harbor. I will bet that a lot of them are surprised when Ambrose just is not where its supposed to be according to their chart.

To properly update your charts you need to subscribe to the Local Notice to Mariners. It is a free, weekly publication from the Coast Guard and is a great resource. It gives you the latest information pertaining to the waterways in your district. This includes changes or repairs to any aides to navigation, repair work being done on bridges and security zones setup around fireworks displays, regattas, races or other events. Also included is a section of special notices. It includes information about tagged fish in various studies and what to do if your come across one, dredging and other interesting nautical tid bits. Once a year they publish a supplement which is just packed with great information and best of all, it only takes a phone call to start it coming. (see appendix) The theory in place is to use the Local Notice to Mariners to update your charts weekly. As you can guess, this just does not happen. There are a couple of companies which make a good attempt at providing updated charts, but none are perfect. There are several charting programs for your computer which update their charts for you regularly on line. They are a step in the right direction. Recently, the National Ocean Service, the organization responsible for our NOAA charts announced that they will provide chart updates via E—Mail. Eventually, these updates can be used to automatically update your electronic charts. This would be a great help in keeping the latest information at your finger tips. Whatever works for you is best. Just remember, that more often than not, there are discrepancies between your chart and the real world.

When going to new locations, you should supplement your charts with a United States Coast Pilot for your area. It is a book, much like a cruising guide, published by the National Ocean Service. The Coast Pilot describes in words and pictures the nuances of each location that you will be navigating through. It is packed with local knowledge and tips, such as where the deep water is and if you should hug the starboard or port side of a particular channel to avoid shoaling. A cruising guide, like The Waterways Guide Series, is all the above plus a restaurant and marina guide. It also costs a lot more than a Coast Pilot. They both should include information which is up to date and it should jive with your chart. If it does not, most likely your chart needs updating. Write the correct information in pencil directly on the chart. Refer to these things as needed to keep the areas you are transiting fresh in your mind. Sometimes however, you need a bit more than these can give. That is when you stop at a marina or gas dock and ask. What you will get is true local knowledge that is worth its weight in gold.

Another great and very inexpensive ($2.50) government publication is Chart No. 1. It is not a chart at all, but basically a legend to explain all the symbols, abbreviations and terms you will find on a chart. I do not think there has ever been a time when I did not open up a chart and learn something new. Sit down at the kitchen table on the next rainy day with a chart, Chart No. 1 and the Coast Pilot and get lost in it for a while. Better yet, do it on your boat. One of my favorite pastimes is to go to the marina with a cup of coffee and partake in this ritual. There's an education to be had in them. Use it to your advantage.

An adjunct to good old fashioned paper charts, which by the way never breakdown or go on the fritz, is a nice chart plotter. It is an electronic device which makes use of the U.S. Department of Defense's Global Positioning System (GPS) to place your vessel on a screen with a chart of the area superimposed over it. What it can do is place your vessel on the chart in a dynamic fashion so that your vessel stays in the center of the screen and the chart moves around you. The most recent one I purchased came with cables to hook it up to my computer at home. It allows me to download enhancements as well as chart corrections so I am always up to date.

The Global Positioning System is comprised of 21 active and three spare satellites orbiting the earth. Your onboard GPS receiver uses three or more satellites to get a fix on your current position. This system is so accurate, that early on, the Department of Defense actually had to degrade the signal, in what they called Selective Availability. This was done so that it could not be used by terrorists for their benefit or in any way compromise national security. The signal was guaranteed to place you within 100 meters, or 328 feet, of your actual position. In a bit of political wrangling, the Coast

Guard developed a fix for this degradation called Differential GPS (DGPS). By using a DGPS unit, your accuracy was then guaranteed to be within 8-20 meters (28-66 feet). As of May 1, 2000, President Clinton ordered that Selective Availability be turned off, giving us three times better accuracy without the use of a DGPS unit. Then in the next most recent advancement, thanks to our friends in the aviation industry, the Wide Area Augmentation System (WAAS) was developed. WAAS, as alluded to above, was developed primarily for pilots who needed a greater degree of accuracy for navigation and precision instrument landings. The system, upon completion, will consist of 22 ground reference stations. These stations will transmit correction signals to the GPS satellites, which will then retransmit the new signal to your onboard GPS. Soon WAAS technology will be a basic part of all new GPS units. My unit is now so accurate, that when I turn it on in the marina it just about has me centered in my slip. Remember though, this is controlled by the government and can be shut down or turned on without notice. Historically, certain areas have never enjoyed even the use of Selective Availability, like the waters around the United Nations in New York. In the turbulent times we are living, predicting the future is not possible. GPS is therefore now, more than ever, an adjunct, not a replacement for your paper charts, associated books and reference materials.

Now that you are safely out of the marina, into the channel and have a good idea of where you are going, the next aspect of boating becomes apparent. You need to know how to interact with other boats safely. This includes knowing how to handle your boat properly. Lets start with the rules of the road. Many years ago the Inter Governmental Maritime Consultative Organization met to establish rules to help prevent collisions at sea. Up until this time there were basically no internationally accepted guidelines for operating a vessel of any size. The result of this meeting in 1972 were the International Regulations for Preventing Collisions at Sea or the 72

COLREGS. They were further broken down into International Regulations and Inland Regulations. There are also separate rules covering the Western Rivers and the Great Lakes.

We will concern ourselves here with the inland rules. These apply inside or shoreward of the COLREG demarcation lines on our charts. You will see a broken magenta line with the words COLREG demarcation line written along it. Inland of this line the Inland rules apply and seaward of this line the International Rules apply. These rules address situations between two vessels only. Three or more vessels coming together constitute a special situation and are not covered by these rules. Also, the rules state that you may depart from these rules at any time to avoid immediate danger. They discuss basically three situations. The first is a meeting situation. That is when two vessels are approaching each other head to head. The preferred manner of passing is for each vessel to alter their course to starboard and pass port to port.

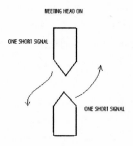

To do this properly you must sound one short blast of 1-2 seconds duration on your whistle (the term whistle will always be used, it refers to your horn). This means, I intend to alter my course to starboard for a port to port passing. The other vessel, if in agreement, should sound one short whistle blast in acknowledgment. If for some reason they are not in agreement, they would sound the danger/doubt signal of five short rapid blasts. You should not pass until whistle signals are agreed upon. Your other choice, while not preferred, is to sound two signals. This means that I intend to alter my course to port and pass you starboard to starboard. Again you should get a like response in order to pass.

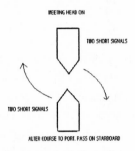

The next situation is overtaking. That is when one vessel is intending to pass another vessel. The vessel being overtaken is called the stand on vessel and is required by the rules to maintain course and speed. The vessel overtaking is called the give way vessel and must stay clear of the vessel being overtaken. Additionally, the give way vessel is required to sound whistle signals to inform the overtaken vessel of its intentions. One short blast means that I intend to overtake you on your starboard side and a like response is expected.

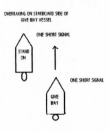

Two short blasts means that I intend to overtake you on your port side and again, a like response is expected.

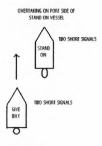

If anyone is in doubt, five short blasts on the whistle signals this doubt and new signals must be proposed. Interestingly, this is the one situation where a sailboat under sail does not have the right of way over a powerboat if it is the overtaking vessel. The sailboat is the give way vessel and must alter course, while the powerboat being overtaken is the stand on vessel and is required to maintain course and speed.

The last possibility we will discuss is a crossing situation. This is a situation which does not meet the definition of meeting or overtaking. The vessel to starboard always has the right of way and is the stand on vessel. That is to say, the vessel on the right always maintains course and speed. While the vessel to the left, or port, is the give way vessel. It is required to keep out of the way of the stand on vessel and must avoid crossing in front. Basically, the give way vessel must alter course and/or speed and cross astern of the stand on vessel. The give way vessel again must signal intent by sounding the appropriate whistle signal. One short blast: I intend to alter course to starboard. A like response is also necessary.

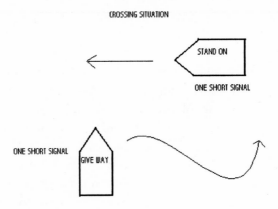

Also, keep in mind that you are allowed to deviate from these rules to avoid immediate danger. Most commercial vessels make these arrangements by VHF radio. The ship to ship channel in most areas is channel 13. The next time you are near a busy port, listen for a while and you will see that these exchanges really do occur. An example of such an exchange usually on channel 13 or 16 is, "Inbound freighter in Thimble Shoal Channel approaching Red 6. This is outbound Tug; Friendship". A common answer might be: "Friendship, this is inbound freighter; Queen of the East". "Queen of the East, I would like to pass on one whistle". "Friendship, one whistle it is, have a safe trip, Queen of the East, Out". "Same to you, Friendship, Out". Here Friendship hailed Queen of the East and established a passing of port to port. No horns were actually sounded, but each intention was understood. These exchanges are very rarely followed by pleasure boaters, but really should be for safety sake.

The full rules are available in paperback form from the government printing office at a reasonable price and is required to be carried onboard all vessels over 40 feet. It a nice thing to familiarize yourself with and keep around for reference. I have intentionally only scratched the surface here. Please do not get the impression that these are the full rules of the road. A full explanation of the rules are well beyond the scope of this book.

As boating becomes more popular we find the waterways getting more and more congested and because the rules only address situations involving two vessels, we will find that common sense will be our best guide. Most frequently, we will have many boats around us with several different situations occurring at once. It is most important during these times to throttle back to a safe speed for the given situation. This is important for several reasons: obviously to give you time to evaluate what others are doing and to allow things to unfold in front of you. You do however, want to have power available to you because at times, a course change is not always enough to avoid a collision. You need speed in certain situations to help you to get out of the way. This speed must be available to you. The only way that it is there if you need it, is if you have slowed down in the first place. Another reason to decrease your speed is because not only are you responsible for your boats actions, but you are responsible for your wake too. You should always try to be aware of the wake you are throwing and where it is going. Are there small boats around which could be swamped? Do not forget boats which are anchored up on a beach and also the shoreline. The shoreline in most areas takes a lot of abuse from boat wakes. Erosion and deterioration could affect the habitats of many forms of wildlife. In many areas you should bring your boat off plane and back into its displacement mode to bring your wake down in size. This must be done early enough to allow your residual wake to dissipate, well before it impacts upon these critical areas.

Generally, in open and deep water, where there is a lot of boat traffic, I like to get up on plane early on, well before entering such an area. Then I back off the throttle so that I am at that point where I am still on plane, but just at that point where moving the throttle back a touch drops you off plane and slows you quickly. Conversely, nudging the throttle forward gives you a quick burst of speed to move you out of harms way rapidly. This gives you a lot of control, visibility and options. Just make sure you are not going too fast for the situation at hand. The only problem with this speed is that many boats tend to throw a large wake, so be aware of your surroundings.

The most dangerous time for a boater is when a planing boat is moving between the displacement mode, where it is shoving water ahead and the planing mode, where the boat is skimming along on top of the water. This is termed getting out of the hole and for good reason. Some boats, usually those underpowered or overloaded, will experience a huge amount of bow rise and it may take a long time to come back down. The captain may have several seconds where he is not able to see over the bow. This can be extremely dangerous. When you do come back down, the whole scene around you may have changed. Recently, a jet skier in my area was killed when a powerboat crushed him while in this awkward, bow up position. Other boaters and jet skiers just do not realize that your visibility is decreased. Not surprisingly, the captain said that he never saw him. He just heard the noise and realized something terrible had happened.

There are several things you can do to improve your boat's performance in these situations. Boats accumulate a lot of weight in extra gear over the years. Spend some time and get rid of what you no longer need and try to keep some of the weight forward. Pump out any water that has accumulated in the bilge before you go out. Also, try not to overload your boat with too many people. Trim the engines all the way in to start and then once up on plane, bring out the engine a bit by depressing the trim up button.

This will adjust your planing attitude to a position you feel will give optimal performance. This position will make your boat as responsive as possible and give you the best fuel economy as well. You can also use your trim tabs, if you have them to level the boat port to starboard. This helps with handling too. Make minor adjustments to correct for uneven weight distribution, but make sure that you do not over adjust. The worst thing you can do is to force the bow down too far. This will cause the boat to bow steer, a situation which makes the boat move in unwanted directions very quickly and unexpectedly. Additionally, make sure your hull is clean and free of growth and accumulations.

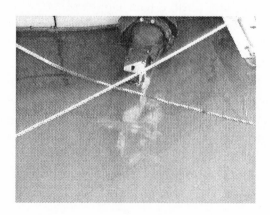

This creates a lot of drag and greatly affects the dynamics of your boat. Lastly, your mechanic may help by tuning up your engine or modifying your outdrive. One of the greatest modifications available for stern drives and outboards, are planing fins. They get installed on the cavitation plate of the engine's lower unit. They help you to get out of the hole much quicker by increasing lift while minimizing drag. They also provide greater stability, better steering control and allow you to stay on plane at a much lower RPM. If you are experiencing problems getting out of the hole, definitely try to address it one way or another because it is downright dangerous.

There are some general rules of thumb you should know about and follow. Some are basic: like always give a sailboat, that is proceeding under sail, the right of way (unless they are overtaking you). This means, keep away from them and give them room to maneuver. Any vessel which may be having difficulty maneuvering should be given the right of way as well. You should avoid crossing in front of another vessel if it may impede its progress or risk a collision. Also, very importantly, when you alter course to avoid a boat in front of you, be certain that you are aware of what is behind you. There are no rear view or side view mirrors on boats, you must physically turn around and look. You must be sure that you are not creating another close quarters situation by your actions. That is to say, do not avoid one close call and cause another. The pecking order is an established hierarchy of vessels having the right of way over others. Briefly, less maneuverable vessels are given priority. Starting at the top are Vessels Not Under Command; that is a vessel, which through some exceptional circumstance, is unable to maneuver. Next are vessels which are Restricted in their Ability to Maneuver. This includes vessels that due to the nature of their work are unable to keep out of the way of other vessels. This may include a dredge or a vessel laying underwater cable. Next are vessels Constrained by their Draft. This would include freighters or other very big ships. Next are fishing vessels such as trawlers, followed by sailboats and finally powerboats. Generally, keep out of the way of any vessel larger than you or any commercial concern.

Additionally, since the increased terrorist threat, the navy has authorized any of its ships to fire on any boat approaching at a high rate of speed within 500 yards. Once the boat is within 100 yards, the ships officers will decide if lethal action is necessary. The Coast Guard warns that boaters should approach at minimal speed and keep a distance of at least 100 yards. The same distance guidelines are in effect for Nuclear Power Plants or Military Piers. Some areas may never see military vessels, while in other areas they are commonplace. The Lower Chesapeake, for example, is one place you will see everything from Battleships, to Hovercrafts, to Submarines. I was once drift fishing in the area of The Chesapeake Bay Bridge Tunnel when the sultry summer silence was broken by an extremely loud and very clear voice over the VHF. "This is Navy Warship calling the vessel off of my port bow. Exit the area immediately" he repeated the message once more and then there was silence. I am certain that with the definitive tone of the callers voice it was not necessary to ask again. I never saw either the Warship or the boat in question, but the message was well received. Keep away and stay away.

Another item that is very important to mention is the recognition of diver down flags. When a diver is in the water, it is required that they fly a red flag with a diagonal white stripe. In addition, the most correct flag to fly is the International Alpha flag. It is a white and blue flag with a chevron cut into one end. To be completely correct both flags should be flown at all times when a diver is in the water. Most of the time you will only see the red flag with the white stripe. Give these boats a wide berth, that is, do not get too close and slow down to reduce your wake. If a diver is in the water, next to the boat and a large wake hits, it can get very dangerous. Not to mention the effects your propeller can have on the diver himself.

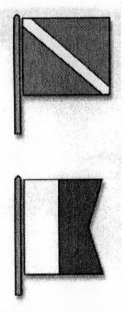

Many of us boat in areas where extremely large vessels transit. Knowing a few things about large vessels, like freighters, will help you to realize that you need to keep away from them at all costs. One problem that they have is that they may take several miles to come to a stop. To do so, they need to shut down their engine and restart it in reverse. This alone can take quite some time. They also have very deep drafts and must stay within the channel to avoid grounding. Assuming they have enough deep water, they still cannot alter their course very quickly. In the case of large freighters, they usually have very high flaring bows that create quite a blind spot for the captain. Sometimes there are blind spots that can extend several hundred feet in front of the vessel. An entire boat can easily disappear from view, so you should not assume that the captain can see you. A good rule of thumb is that if you cannot see the wheelhouse, he will not be able to see you as well. Lastly, large vessels also throw a large bow wave, but even more damaging is the stern wave. It contains a lot of energy and can cause you to lose control. Additionally, a phenomenon called stern suction is a force to be avoided. It causes you to be pulled toward the vessels hull, usually a bit forward of the stern. Sometimes it can even pull a boat under the vessel's hull. Basically, you should do everything in your power to avoid getting close enough to experience it. Do not be afraid to establish communications with these ships. It helps to remove any confusion and the ship's Master will generally appreciate your efforts. Technically, the captain of a ship is referred to as the ship's Master. You can hail them on channel 13 or if necessary on channel 16. An example of such an exchange would be, "this is the Lynn Ann calling the eastbound container ship, Pride of the Orient". On channel 13, when they answer, identify yourself. "I am the white sport fisherman off your starboard bow. I will wait until you are clear and then pass astern of you". They will confirm your intention and then you should proceed. If you hail them on channel 16, ask them to move to a working channel to give them your intentions.

Another immense danger is from barges being towed astern or pushed ahead. Whenever you see a tugboat, look behind it. Sometimes quite far behind it to see if it is towing astern. Tugs use a huge towing line or cable called a hawser. They sometimes let out a half mile or more of cable. This cable is commonly submerged or partially submerged. Never, Never, Never pass between a tug and its barge. The hawser will cause grave damage to you and your vessel. There are many stories of boats contacting a towing hawser at a high rate of speed. The results are always catastrophic, with tales of cabins being ripped off of hulls, sinking and death. The problem is that because of the large distance between the tug and the barge you may falsely think that the two are unrelated. These types of accidents happen often enough and involve both pleasure and commercial vessels, that we must assume it must be difficult to tell that the two are attached by a cable.

Tugs also push barges ahead at times.

This offers the tug a bit more control over its barges, but they need relatively calm water to do this. To give you an idea of size, a tug is usually well over 65 feet and a barge may be over three football fields or 900 feet long. Often many of these are lashed together. This is a massive structure, operating with limited control. Avoid it at all costs.

Boaters often underestimate the speed of a large vessel. They mistakenly think that because they are so big, they are also very slow. A tug traveling at 10 Knots will cover a nautical mile in only 6 minutes. If you are 1000 feet in front of this tug, you only have about one minute to get out of the way. That is really not much time. For your information, the term Knot means nautical miles per hour. A nautical mile is 6080 feet. This corresponds conveniently to the average length of one minute of latitude. A land mile is 5280 feet. Miles per hour refers to land miles and Knots refers to nautical miles.

Thus, one Knot is slightly faster than one Mile Per Hour. It is not correct to say Knots per hour. As a unit of speed, it includes the rate of travel.

There are other hazards on the water which are less imposing than large ships, but need to be avoided never the less. A good example are crab and lobster pot buoys. They are pulled with the current and the line that connects them to the pot, called the warp, may be long. Therefore you should avoid getting too close, lest you get tangled up with one. Several things can happen if you accidentally hit one. Your prop may cut the line or it may wrap around the prop hub and cause your engine to stall. If the latter happens you have some untangling to do. Be careful you do not take a surprise swim. Wear your PFD and if it is too dangerous, call for a tow. Keep another possibility in mind. If you are driving through a minefield of buoys and suddenly experience a loss of power and steering control, you may be dragging a pot. On the Chesapeake Bay I sometimes will use a line of crab pot buoys to guide me to the channel. You have to figure that they need to be placed in fairly deep water to catch crabs, but also to allow for the draft of the boat that tends them. With this assumption, I feel confident that I will not run aground. Well, one day I experienced a sudden loss of power and a bad vibration. Initially, I thought that I blew a piston. As I began limping back to shore, I took a shortcut through an area that I knew only had two feet of water. My small boat only draws eight inched so I was not worried. All of a sudden my son started yelling, "something's following us". I looked back to see a crab pot with some very unhappy crabs in it being pulled along the bottom. After some minor surgery on the warp, we were back in business. Be respectful of the bay men and if you need to cut the warp, retie it and drop it back in. We would rather not abandon traps on the bottom anyway.

Depth finders are an extremely helpful tool both for safety and navigation. Not to mention what they do for fishermen and divers who are attempting to locate fish and various structures. Depth finders help us stay in deep water, but until now, they have had some serious limitations. The main problem is that most of them tell us what the depth of the water is under the boat. Kind of like closing the gate after the horse has already left. What we really need to know is the depth of the water a bit in front of the boat. With improving sonar technology, some of the higher end units have forward scanning capabilities. Unfortunately, unless we want to upgrade we are stuck with what we have. I am sure as the technology improves the cost will come down soon. Never the less, the information you get is valuable. Most units have an alarm to warn you of low water so you do not always need to keep your eye on it. If the alarm sounds, back off on your throttle and if necessary, raise your outboard or stern drive up a little. This will give you more clearance below, but do not raise it past its water intake and make sure that you are discharging that telltale stream of water. If you are on an inboard, you of course cannot raise your running gear and you most definitely do not want to ground. Of all the boats out there, inboards have the most to lose in these situations. If you cannot figure out where deeper water is, first post a lookout in the bow to tell you what they see. Most importantly, if it looks like the water is getting lower, here is where a good pair of polarized sunglasses can come in handy. They enable you to see right through the water. Next, try to head back from the direction you came. Make your turn slowly and in a real pinch, bring some of your passengers forward to raise the stern a little. Try to maintain headway and if you do get stuck do not panic.

Your first instinct may probably be the worst thing you can do, that is, to go into reverse and give it a lot of throttle. This is the same thing that happens when your car gets stuck in the snow. The first thing you do is hit the gas and get yourself stuck deeper. On your boat, this may cause sand to be piled up under the hull and make things worse. Additionally, it may clog your raw water cooling system with sand and it can tear off parts of your running gear. Also, if you have struck hard, first check to see that you are not leaking. If you are, stay stuck. That way you will not sink. Always know the direction of the tide. If its incoming, you may just need to wait a while. If it is outgoing, chances are you will be there for some time.

There is no magic bullet for these situations. Your best bet may be to lighten the load, both people and gear, if it is safe. This will increase buoyancy. Sometimes, moving your passengers forward will raise the stern a bit and allow you to push off if you are not very hard aground. Get an anchor out toward deeper water so large wakes will not lift you and throw you further aground and call for assistance on your VHF. If you act quickly and get off, great. If not, make the call. Whatever the outcome, it is a humbling experience. Your responsibility is to keep it safe. That is what is most important.

Some days just do not turn out as planned in spite of our best efforts. The weather is often to blame. Keep an ear to your weather channel for any changes and keep an eye to the sky. Be leery of those hazy, hot and humid summer days when thunderstorms are likely to kick up. The best place for your boat to be in a thunderstorm is in your marina, securely tied down. The best place for you to be is at home. Heed the warnings or your instinct and head to port before the storm hits. If this is not possible, decide if you can run ahead of the storm to a harbor or cove that will offer you some protection. If you do, anchor up with your largest anchor and pay out a lot of line. We will cover this topic in detail later on. Make sure that as the wind shifts you will not swing into anything. Make a mental note of your surroundings, including distances from various objects. Use this information to determine if your anchor is dragging. Stay alert as to what is going on and wait it out. If you cannot outrun the storm, put your bow into the wind and just stem the current. That is basically, just try to stay in about the same place and keep a good lookout posted. Do this until conditions improve. Fortunately, thunderstorms usually do not last very long. Use your weather radio to confirm that this is true for this particular storm.

One Labor Day a few years ago, Long Island, NY was hit by a line of extremely severe weather which reeked havoc on the Long Island Sound as well as the Great South Bay. There were deaths, capsized boats, groundings and general mayhem. After events like these I like to dissect the outcomes to help us learn from them. Firstly, this storm was not a surprise. It was forecast most of the day and should have been common knowledge. This was one of those times where the forecast was right on the money. People did not want this bad forecast to ruin their last hurrah of the boating season and probably stayed out in spite of what they knew. Secondly, when the storm came in as fast as it did, they should have stayed put rather than try to run. Most people could not have possibly made port. They were running through the storm with a huge number of other boats. This made the risk of collision very great. Additionally, all of the boat wakes made for very confused and dangerous seas. Thirdly, the heavy rains made visibility very poor, yet another reason why staying put was probably the best choice. Fourthly, heavy, gusting winds literally flipped several boats that were running through it at too great a speed. Lastly, the storm surge or buildup of water ahead of the storm caused by the high winds, pushed many boats on shore and when the storm rapidly withdrew, so did the water. These people were left high and dry. It is possible, that in a storm as fierce as this one, nowhere was safe enough. This was one of those situations where the only right thing that you could have done was to stay home. Being the knowledgeable boater that you are you may very well have made that decision.

As this situation demonstrates, the forecast was there. People just needed to listen to it. We therefore do not need to be meteorologists just to enjoy a day on the water. What we need to know is how and where to access the needed information before we go out. I rely on the Internet quite a bit and use several sites (see appendix) for predictions. I also like to access a site which gets me wind speed, wave height and temperature information right off of a buoy weather station. There is no better way to get a feel for the current conditions than this. Well maybe one, I also search the live cam sites and get actual real time pictures of the waters I intend to boat in. The Internet is really a remarkable thing. Use it to your advantage. Once on the water however, you most likely will need to get updated forecasts from the weather stations on your VHF and also learn to become a good observer.

All of the information we have at our finger tips today is only as good as our interpretation of it and our personal fortitude in making a good decision based on it. This includes deciding to leave the dock in the first place or cutting a trip short. One story keeps coming to mind to drive this point home. It is not however, a boating story. Remember John F. Kennedy, Jr's flight from New Jersey to Martha's Vineyard. Conditions were less than ideal. I remember interviews with other pilots who chose not to fly that night. Fog was the main culprit and the area they were flying into was notorious for heavy fog. The other culprit was a later than expected departure, making this a night flight. A significant change for someone inexperienced and not able to fly by instrumentation alone. A short flight or a long car ride were the choices and a lapse in good judgement, along with the desire to not inconvenience anyone, cost three people their lives.

As boaters, we make these decisions every time we go out. We take a chance on a bad forecast because we have planned a particular trip and canceling it would be a big disappointment. Thankfully, our sport is a bit more forgiving than flying but serious injury and death can most definitely occur and it is absolutely more disappointing than a missed or delayed trip. Make a good adult decision based upon all the available data and always err on the side of safety. I always try to have a plan B in place. I tell my kids that if the weather is good, we will go out on a fishing trip. If the weather is bad, we will go to the movies or do something else they enjoy. That way I feel it is easier to make the hard decisions.

If your decision is to go out on the water, then you need to learn to be a good observer. You need to be aware of changes that may signal a decline in the current weather. Keep a constant eye on the clouds. You do not need to know all the different types, just recognize the ominous ones. Anvil shaped thunder heads or cumulonimbus clouds are a good start. Watch the clouds on various days and you will soon begin to formulate your own opinions based on appearance and movement. We are out on the water to stop and smell the roses anyway, so take in the beauty of nature at the same time. Also, keep an eye on the wind, both speed and direction. We want to be alert to changes, such as a shift in the direction or an increase or decrease in velocity. The National Weather Service issues advisories regarding wind. A small craft advisory indicates winds to 33 knots (38 MPH) with corresponding sea conditions which may make operation of small crafts dangerous. This should be a factor in your decision to go or stay. I give a lot of weight to wind as it has a great effect on boat handling and sea conditions. My personal favorite however, is the barometer. It is probably the least used indicator by the recreational boater, but a little information can tell you a great deal about future conditions. Its use is an acquired skill and requires additional information such as changes in wind speed and direction, temperature and cloud formation. A Barometer measures changes in atmospheric pressure. Generally, a steady barometer means the current weather will continue. A rising barometer means fair weather is building and a falling barometer signals approaching poor weather. Barometric readings are given with the weather forecast on your VHF's weather band, or better yet mount a small barometer on your boat or at home. Remember, the barometer is used as an adjunct to a forecast only. If you are planning a long day on the water and the weather appears to be fair, take a look at the barometer. If it is falling, you may need to rethink your activities or at the very least keep a more vigilant eye to the sky.

So now we are navigating like the pro's, dealing with boat traffic, watching the weather and avoiding obstacles. Most of our driving behavior at sea will center around avoidance. We desperately try to avoid other boats, obstructions, low water etc. On boats, we have to be basically defensive drivers. In our cars we are mostly offensive drivers. You cannot operate a boat with the same mind set that you operate a car. There are just too many other factors that exist that are out of your control. You must spend time evaluating situations, backing off and allowing them time to develop. Proceed with caution and soon we will be approaching our destination. Arriving safely is a big plus. Staying put once we get there is another issue. Next, we will cover the usual methods of keeping our boat stationary while we enjoy what we came out to do. We need to do this efficiently and courteously so we can get on with the fun.

Chapter 5

STAYING PUT

Wise men learn by other men's
mistakes, fools by their own
— *H.G. Bohn*

Whether we have planned to go fishing, picnic on the beach, raft up with some friends, relax in a lazy anchorage or have lunch in a waterside restaurant, a plan of attack is crucial. On this hypothetical day we will do all of these things. This will give us the opportunity to learn how to deal with our boat in all possible situations.

In addition to a plan, we need to have the proper gear for the job at hand. Anchoring may seem very straight forward to you, just drop the hook and do what you want. However, to perform this task properly and efficiently, it is more of an art than a science.

As I have mentioned previously, I like to spend time vacationing in a campground on the Chesapeake Bay. After many years renting a small aluminum boat, I decided to build the ultimate skiff for crabbing, fishing and clamming in that area. Well, as usual with boating, my two thousand dollar expenditure turned into a ten thousand dollar skiff to end all other skiff's. When complete however, it was exactly what I wanted. I launched it from its trailer, for the first time, into the Chesapeake one afternoon. It was to stay in the water, anchored up off of my campsite for a full week. As usual, in that area, only a couple of hours after launching the sky darkened and a fierce storm approached. I knew it was likely because NOAA weather was predicting a 75% chance of late afternoon thunderstorms and the pattern the week before was a short storm everyday at five in the afternoon. Well, this was no short thunderstorm. The wind within minutes approached 50 MPH. It rained buckets and lasted for two hours. I spent the entire time standing at the window of my camper questioning every decision I ever made while building this boat. Is the bilge pump powerful enough to handle the load? Are the cleats fastened with large enough bolts? Is the weight distributed properly so it will not capsize? As well as a hundred more. The one thing I was not worried about was if it would break anchor and drift away with the five foot seas that had built. I was not worried because I always anchor the same way. This is the way I will teach you in the next few pages. If you always do it the same way, you will perfect your technique and be confident that you are doing things in a time tested proven way that will not fail you.

After the storm passed, I waded out to the boat to assess the damage. Not only did the boat make it through this severe storm, it weathered it perfectly. As the sky turned fiery red and bright orange, the clouds began to break, guaranteeing a beautiful sunset. I stood in the bow enjoying the cooler, dryer air that the storm had left behind. The sky continued to fill with color, the hull slapped the water ever so gently and that very moment was the greatest boating experience of my life. A high I strive to replicate as often as possible.

The gear you carry to anchor your boat is collectively known as the ground tackle. It consists of an anchor, a length of chain and line. The chain and line when attached to an anchor is known as the rode. When choosing an anchor you need to consider several factors. The size of the boat is very important as is the size of the boat's above the water structures. The higher the boat, the larger the sail area and the greater the effect the wind will have on the boat. The type of bottom you will generally be anchoring in is critical. One anchor may not be suitable for all bottoms. By far the most common anchor found on recreational boats is the Danforth.

It was invented in 1938 by Richard Danforth and has proven itself time and time again as a general purpose anchor. Some advantages are that they can be fairly lightweight and still provide a great deal of holding power. They are easy to set and easy to retrieve. Additionally, they can be stored neatly in an onboard storage locker or right on the bow pulpit. Disadvantages include offering a poor hold in grassy or rocky bottoms. Be careful when shopping for one. There are many which are of poorer quality and may not perform reliably in all situations.

Other less commonly used anchors are the plow type which is very effective in grasses, weeds, sand and mud.

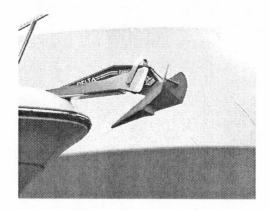

However, its use in heavy grasses is questionable. It requires a longer length of chain than other anchors, and is a bit awkward and hard to stow. A bow roller on a pulpit is the best place to keep it. The claw anchor is similar to the plow, but is of one piece construction. It is a reliable anchor in many bottoms and is said to work well in gravel bottoms. Grapnel anchors are not suggested for general purpose use, but they are good in rocky bottoms. They are used mostly by fishermen who anchor over rocks or wrecks. They are difficult to dislodge and you usually must apply enough force to bend a tine to retrieve them. Sometimes you must resign yourself to the fact that you must lose them entirely.

Choose your anchors by first looking at a chart of the areas you will be boating in. The bottom types are marked on the chart and refer to Chart number 1 to decipher their abbreviations. Generally, if you are boating in areas that are not very rocky or do not have heavy grasses, a Danforth is your best bet. Carrying two anchors is mandatory. These should be fully rigged and ready to go. I have an oversized Danforth stored on a bow roller with a rode of chain and three strand nylon line. My second anchor is exactly the same, only stored in a deck locker. If I spent time boating in rocky areas, I would keep a rigged Grapnel anchor on board. Local knowledge is important in this regard. Ask at the marina or boat supply store for suggestions. Also, see what is hanging off the bows of the boats in a local marina.

Your rode is very important to the success of your technique. A length of chain attached to the anchor is imperative for many reasons. It offers good resistance to abrasion as it sits on the bottom. Barnacle covered rocks, oyster shells etc. can cause chaffing on a nylon line and lead to a failure. Equally important, as it lays along the bottom, it provides a more horizontal pull on the anchor, which regardless of type is necessary for a good hold. I have read a few different theories regarding the appropriate length of chain you should use. Some feel you should calculate length according to the boats length. This does not make a lot of sense to me because you could have a completely open 24' boat that is influenced very little by the wind or you could have a 24' boat with a large superstructure and flying bridge. The latter will pull very hard on an anchor in a heavy wind and will require a longer length of chain to keep this pull on the anchor more horizontal. Another theory suggests a relationship should exist between the weight of the anchor and the weight of the chain. I feel that anchor weight may not be all that important. Mostly because once the anchor is set, the weight of the anchor is not a big issue anymore. What is most important is that when force is applied to an anchor, it must be done so as close to horizontal as possible. This makes sense when you realize that to raise an anchor a vertical force is best. So how much chain do you need? Well, that must then depend upon the length of the rode that you are using. Your length of rode is figured depending upon the depth of the water. This ratio of length of rode to depth of water is known as Scope. Because we cannot conveniently change our chain when we change our Scope, we need some general rules. Basically, the longer the rode the longer the chain. Come up with an average water depth for your boating area and size your length of chain accordingly. This length is based upon the average length of rode you will be using. Use 6'-8' of chain for rodes up to 100', 10'-12' of chain for rodes up to 150' and 15'-20' of chain for rodes over 200'.

Using a scope of 5:1 or 7:1 (length of rode : for every 1 foot of water depth) is normally suggested for calm water. A scope of 10:1 is preferred for stormy weather. I generally use a scope of 8:1 for all circumstances and have never had problems. To figure out the ideal amount of rode to pay out, you should consult your depth finder for the current depth of the water. Then if your bow rises far above the water, add this distance to the depth of the water, as this is where the anchor rode will be tied off. For example, if your bow is 10' above the waterline and you are in 20' of water, for a scope of 8:1 you need to pay out 240' of rode not 160'. That is a big difference, especially if a storm kicks up.

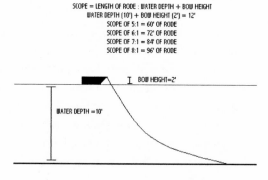

SCOPE = LENGTH OF RODE : WATER DEPTH + BOW HEIGHT
WATER DEPTH (10') + BOW HEIGHT (2') = 12'
SCOPE OF 5:1 = 60' OF RODE
SCOPE OF 6:1 = 72' OF RODE
SCOPE OF 7:1 = 84' OF RODE
SCOPE OF 8:1 = 96' OF RODE

BOW HEIGHT=2'

WATER DEPTH =10'

If you are anchoring for an extended period of time you also need to factor in tidal differences. This information can be found in the Coast Pilot or usually on your chart. Figure your greatest possible depth by adding the tidal difference to your depth if it is low tide. Do not add anything if it is high tide and add a portion if it is between tides. An exact number is not necessary. This is not brain surgery. These numbers are most important in areas with huge tidal differences such as Nova Scotia where the tide may rise and fall thirty or forty feet. If you do a lot of overnighting, a great low tech product to have on hand is an old fashioned lead line, commonly called a Nantucket Sounder. It consists of a bronze weight and a knotted line. You drop it to the bottom and count the knots to give you the water depth and bow height at the same time. Some lead lines also have a hole in the weight which can be filled with Vaseline, chewing gum or any other sticky substance. This material will bring up a piece of the bottom so you can see exactly what you are anchoring in. The high tech version of a lead line is a handheld depth finder. They look like a small flashlight with an LED screen. Just point it down and it tells you the distance to the bottom. Unfortunately, it cannot tell you what the bottom consists of.

You can measure the amount of rode you are putting out in a number of ways. You could estimate the width of your arms when they are apart and count up the feet as you let line out, or you could use a line counter which is a device that the line feeds through and counts off the feet as the line goes overboard. The more traditional way is to mark the line with colored thread at specified distances. The only problem is that you need to remember what each color thread means. Some people are now using different colored cable ties to mark distances, but again the older we get the less we remember. I prefer to use printed rode markers. They are sold usually in 30' increments and have printed numbers on them. You will never have to guess what distance that particular color stands for.

A final note about your anchor rode is that you should use nylon line which is attached to your chain with a shackle. Make sure the shackle's locking pin is secured with stainless steel locking wire or a plastic cable tie.

This prevents the locking pin from backing out and leaving your anchor behind. Also lock the shackle that attaches the chain to the anchor. Nylon line is used because of its elastic nature which provides a substantial shock absorbing role to give you a smoother ride when at anchor. When your nylon line gets hard to handle from too many dunkings in salt water you can wash them in your clothes washing machine with fabric softener. They will feel and handle great. Also, do not forget to tie off the bitter end of the rode somewhere before dropping your anchor overboard. Many an anchor has met the bottom on a permanent basis because of this oversight.

Anchoring without a windlass (a winch) is best accomplished by two people. The area should be chosen carefully. An important thing to consider is your swing. Allow enough room between other boats, buoys, piers and shallow water for your boat to swing. Add the length of your boat to the length of the rode and that is a ball park estimate of the distance you could swing. Of course, you will swing farther at low tide than you will at high tide. If all the boats in an anchorage are on one hook (using one anchor off of the bow) you would think they will all swing in unison. Well, that is not necessarily true. A lot of factors are involved when a boat swings at anchor. Such as wind, current, draft, keels, sail area and a multitude of other factors. Therefore, keep away from all obstacles.

Start by bringing the boat into the area, against the current and to a stop in your desired position. Allow the boat to drop off sternward and then drop the anchor to the bottom. Once down, continue allowing the boat to drift with the current 30' or so and tie off the rode. This will usually cause the anchor to grab the bottom. If it sets, the line will tighten and the boat will hold. If this does not happen untie the line and drop off more. Tie off again, at this point the anchor should have a good bite. Sometimes giving the boat a shot of reverse throttle will really set the anchor well. Once you are holding to your satisfaction, drop off once again to the desired scope. Tie off to the bow cleat or chock and make a visual check of the area. Use an object, preferably a stationary one to get a mental fix on your position. If possible, use two or more objects and refer to them from time to time to make sure your position is not changing. Many GPS's have drift alarms that can be set to alert you to a change in your position. These are great for overnighters. If you do find that you are dragging your anchor, you may have calculated your scope improperly or you need a greater scope for the situation you are in. If this does not solve the problem, retrieve the anchor and make sure it is not fouled. If it is not, the problem may be the type of anchor that you are using for this particular bottom. You may need to change anchor types or change location.

Some people like to set two anchors, typically this is done as a safety measure and to limit swing. There are many ways to do this. Fishermen who like to anchor up over wrecks will commonly use a bow and a stern anchor so that their boat will remain in position over their favorite honey spot. If this is done, the sea conditions must be perfect, as this holds the boat in a very unnatural position relative to the waves. It can be at risk of swamping if the seas are abeam or astern. Some people prefer to use two anchors off the bow. They set one, then carefully motor ahead and set another. Ideally the angle between them should be close to 45 degrees.

2 ANCHORS OFF THE BOW
THEY SHOULD BE AT LEAST 45 DEGREES APART

This set up will limit your swing and offer you the added protection of two anchors. Yet others try to reduce swing even more by setting up what is called a Bahamian Mooring. This is when two anchors are set out 180 degrees from one another with the boat in the center.

BAHAMIAN MOORING
2 ANCHORS SET 180 DEGREES APART

One anchor is set and then twice your desired scope is let out. The second is dropped once the boat gets to the full distance of this double scope. Then the first anchor's rode is hauled in by half. While hauling in this extra rode, stop about half way and allow the second anchor to set. Snug up both anchor lines and you are set. The advantages here, as previously said, include decreasing swing considerably, giving the added security of having two anchors out and if you will experience a tide change, the anchors will not have to reset themselves when the current reverses. The disadvantage is that if the area has heavy boat traffic, the risk of fouling with another boat is greater.

The last item involves retrieving your ground tackle properly so that it does not get damaged and so that you do not get hurt. Assuming still that you do not have a windlass, there are several ways to undo what you have just done so well. Always start and warm up your engine before you do anything else. The last thing you want to have happen is to haul in the anchor and find out that you have a dead battery and cannot start up. If you have a helper, station him at the bow and motor up until the boat is directly over the anchor. Make sure your helper hauls in the slack line as you go. Then have him tie off the rode once again and motor past the anchor to break it free. Pull in the remaining rode and anchor and you are all set. Make sure before he leaves the bow that he stows all the gear safely. If you hit a wave, you do not want the anchor or rode or both going overboard. The resultant flotsam will invariably foul your prop and cause all kinds of problems. If you are doing this alone, you will not have the luxury of motoring up to the anchor and you must use muscle to haul in the rode. In smaller boats you may be able to bring the rode to the boats starboard side and motor ahead and haul in the slack at the same time. The more civilized method of anchor handling on larger boats is by use of a windlass

A windlass is a special type of winch which can be manual or motor driven. Manual windlasses are an adjunct to muscle power, offering the user a mechanical advantage and are either lever type, employing a back and forth motion, or vertical axis which requires a circular motion. Electric windlasses drop and haul your anchor with the touch of a button. The advantages, of course, include saving your back and hands, but also in rough seas a crew member need not venture out to the bow. Windlasses can handle rodes of rope and chain and usually stow the rode neatly below in your anchor locker. They also secure your anchor on a bow pulpit. All of this can be done remotely from the helm.

Windlasses are chosen for your boat based upon the vessels weight and the type of bottom most commonly encountered. Rocky bottoms generally require a stronger pull to heave the anchor and therefore, you need a more powerful windlass to do the job. When hauling in the rode you should always use the boats engine to motor up to the anchor. You should not use the windlass to pull the boat as it creates excessive strain on its electric motor. Also, because it draws a lot of current, the engine should always be running while operating the windlass so you do not drain the battery.

Whatever setup you have, you need to perform a visual check of your ground tackle and related gear twice a season. Check the nylon line for signs of chafe and rinse it with fresh water to keep it flexible. Check your shackle pins to make sure they are still locked down and tight. Check out all other components of your ground tackle system to make sure it is not ready to fail on you. If you have a windlass, check the owners manual for any suggested service it may need. These little items will keep your gear working flawlessly for many years.

Remember, that while at anchor, you may be required to display an anchor light or day shape. An anchor light is an all around white light which must be placed high enough to be seen without interference from things like Bimini tops or radar arches. It must be displayed at night or during times of restricted visibility, such as in fog or during storms. The day shape that is required to be shown if necessary, is a ball. Vessels under 164 feet (50 meters) at anchor must display one all around anchor light while vessels over this size must display two. Vessels under 65 feet (20 meters) need not display an anchor light if anchored in a Special Anchorage as designated on your chart. They must, however, display an anchor light at all other locations. Vessels under 23 feet (7 meters) not anchored in or near a channel, fairway or where vessels normally navigate need not display an anchor light or day shape.

These are the rules, but let common sense be your guide. If you are anchored at night and feel that you may not be seen, turn on your light. A reasonably good battery can withstand a single bulb burning for a considerable period of time. Even in a secluded cove you never know who might be passing by in the middle of the night. Your light will break the darkness and make you visible. There are many reasons for people to be out on the water. We are generally out for pleasure and tend to use the water mostly during the day. If we are out at night, most of the time we are anchored up and asleep. Other people use the water for work and are routinely out all night or start their day well before first light. Keep this in mind when choosing the place you want to anchor and how you plan to keep your vessel visible while you are resting.

Another popular pastime is rafting. This summertime ritual is when a group of boaters plan to get together at a specific place to tie up side to side and socialize. The first boat to arrive anchors up with their largest hook, set to the appropriate scope. As each subsequent boat arrives they just tie up to the next in line. Each boat should put out as many fenders as possible to protect one another. Align the boats so that any rigging will not cause interference with another boat. This applies mostly to sail boats. Tie up cleat to cleat, leaving a bit of slack to allow each boat to move independently. Try to keep the anchored boat in the center of the developing raft and drop more hooks if necessary depending upon the conditions. If you plan to stay rafted after dark or overnight, be sure to light all the boats with anchor lights.

Make sure that someone keeps an eye out to make sure that you do not drag anchor during the night, especially if the wind picks up or shifts. Rafting lends itself to partying. Keep in mind that even though you may not have plans to operate your boat until the next day, things may change. The anchor may drag and not reset or a severe storm may kick up requiring you to break up the raft. Make sure you designate a competent driver and good decision maker for each boat. Let this person operate the boat if it becomes necessary and decide upon the course of action to be taken. This rule should be strict and adhered to always.

Yet another great boating experience is spending time at the beach. Once again, the key to making this pleasurable and not frustrating is to have a plan. I use my small skiff a lot to get to the beach. Its definitely convenient but still needs to be anchored up the same way as much larger boats. I always avoid beaching this boat even though it is small and fairly light. I once let the tide drop, which left it high and dry. I erroneously thought I could push it off the beach when I was ready to leave. This boat has a flat bottom and it created a sort of suction in the sand, I could not budge it an inch to save my life. No matter what hull style you have, dead weight is hard to move. When and if you do get it moving, sand piles up behind the hull and you end up needing to move a portion of the earth to refloat it. After this experience, I now think of beaching as intentional grounding. If I do not want to ground anywhere else; why do it here on purpose?

Your approach to the beach will depend upon where this particular beach is located. One of my favorite haunts is on a very crowded inlet. There are both swells from the ocean and wakes from the heavy boat traffic in the area. In this situation I approach the beach by backing perpendicular to the shore. I drop an anchor off the bow and let out enough rode to allow me to continue backing up toward the beach, trimming the engine up as I go. I do this until I am in about 2 feet of water and shut down the engine. This should give me plenty of water under my keel when the engine is fully raised. If your boat draws more water than say, 18 inches then you need to stay in deeper water. The idea here being, get as close to shore as possible to easily unload your passengers and their gear without damaging your running gear. I have a person stationed at the stern with an anchor tied off to a stern cleat. Make sure he has enough rode to get the anchor up onto the beach. When I have the boat as close as possible to shore and the engine is shut down I have this person enter the water. He keeps tension on the rode as he walks the anchor to the beach and sets it by hand in the sand.

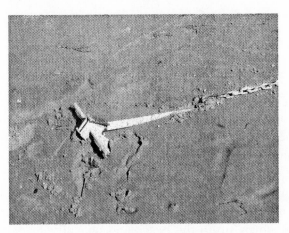

The bow anchor prevents the boat from moving shoreward while this person is entering the water. This time however, is the most dangerous time in the process. Keep in mind that your nylon rode stretches and if a wave hits the boat with this person or anyone close by they are in danger of being hit by the boat. Enter the water only when it looks calm and move away from the boat immediately.

After the passengers and gear is off loaded, you can easily adjust the two anchors until you are in deeper water just by letting out more rode on one end and pulling in the excess on the other. This arrangement keeps your boats stern to the beach which allows the waves to be taken by the bow. The best part of this setup is that if you need to make adjustments to the boat due to tidal changes, it can usually be done without having to reset an anchor.

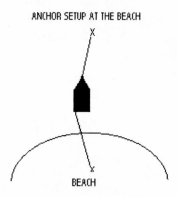

ANCHOR SETUP AT THE BEACH

BEACH

Make sure that you are in deep enough water so that the boat does not bottom out in the trough of a wave. Wade in to shore and have fun.

If the beach is more secluded or in an area where there is minimal wave action and light boat traffic, you may choose to just use one anchor off the bow. Typically, you can nose the boat slowly up to the beach and unload your passengers and gear while one person, in the water, holds the boat steady. Then either walk the anchor out to a depth which will accommodate the boats draft or power the boat out and drop the hook. Either way, pay out enough rode to be safe and wade into the beach yourself. Keep an eye on the boat to make sure that the wind and current keep it from beaching itself and enjoy the day. If you find that the boat wants to migrate to shore, you will have no choice but to use an additional anchor off the stern to keep it in place.

You have one other option to avoid all of this work and believe me, at times it really can be work to do this properly. Also, if your boat is on the larger size or has a straight inboard with its running gear hanging below the hull, you can anchor up a bit off the beach and use a dinghy to come ashore. A lot of people use an inflatable raft for this purpose. Others tow a dinghy to their destination. Whatever you choose, the goal here is to gain access to another source of enjoyment for you and your family. This needs to be done according to plan so as to avoid stress. That is one reason why we use the water, to feel the stresses flow from our bodies. Think about what you are going to do ahead of time and all will be well.

Leaving the beach is simply the same process in reverse. Make sure that your seaward anchor is left set as you are loading. If the boat needs to be pulled closer to the beach to make things easier, just let out more rode from the seaward anchor. When you are all loaded, use this anchor to hold you in place and pull in some rode to until you have enough water to start your engine. Once you are started and confident that you are operating properly, then and only then, pull in the last anchor and off you go.

Some additional things to keep in mind when pulling up to a beach include; Posting a lookout when approaching the shore to help avoid things like rocks and submerged pilings or the like. Also, avoid letting the hull rub against the sand for very long. The sand will act just like sandpaper and will rub off your bottom paint. This of course will cause it to lose its effectiveness. This will lead to growth on the hull and both performance and gas milage will suffer. Lastly, try to avoid getting too close to other boats. It is very difficult to control a boats movement by holding onto it when it is close to shore. Breaking waves, even very small ones, have a lot of power in them and therefore have a great effect on the boat. Waves rarely hit the beach exactly parallel and because of this can easily push you sideways. Leave plenty of room between you and the next guy to avoid problems.

Yet another way people spend the day is to enjoy a meal at their favorite waterfront restaurant. I know of several places where the food may be great but the views are even better. One of my all time favorites is in Maryland. I have eaten there many times and each time I go it is better than the time before. What I really enjoy is watching boats of all sizes approach the dock and back into a slip. What better way to learn about boat handling but to watch it first hand. This particular restaurant attracts some very large boats from all over the east coast. While backing a large boat with precision is no easy task. You must realize that the sheer size of some of these vessels is also what helps them. What I mean is that they may be less affected by wind and current than a smaller boat. They also may have twin screws or other devices which help them to maneuver, such as bow thrusters.

Now do not get the wrong idea. These boats are still affected by wind and current. It just may take longer to notice that effect than on a smaller boat. Additionally, there are more ways to counter these effects. There also is a lot more at stake however, if a problem arises. Some of these boats are 50 feet or more and there is no easy way to just shut down the engines and use boat hooks to pull them in if needed.

I just feel, that at times, the operator of a small boat has a harder time than the operator of a larger vessel. This is apparent when you sit and watch boats dock in a setting like this for a while. What it does not mean is that people operating smaller boats are less experienced than operators of larger boats. All it means is that the person who owns a smaller boat likes a boat of that size for a particular reason and visa versa. I know a guy that operates a 110 foot boat for a living and has a 24 foot boat for pleasure. It is definitely not because he cannot or is afraid to handle a large boat. It is simply what he enjoys.

So you choose a nice restaurant for lunch. As you

approach, try to see if there is a slip available which can accommodate your boat. Some places require that you contact them on a specific VHF channel before you dock. This information can be obtained from a cruising guide or sometimes a sign is posted. Try to look for it on this first pass. Usually you need to back into these slips. Motor past once or twice and note the direction of the wind and current. If possible, you want to back in against the current. This requires you to approach with the current so when you slow and begin to back you will be against it. This will give you the most control. When you make your approach to the slip, do so slowly and try to place the stern as close to the slip as possible. It is at this time that the effects of wind and current will be most noticeable. Use reverse to help counter their effects and back toward the slip. Speed is not important. Maintain only enough stern way to give you control. This will give you time to make minor adjustments with the steering wheel. There is no need to be a purest and do this without any assistance. Station one or two people at the stern with boat hooks. Tell them to use them to fend off of things if necessary and only use them to pull you in if you tell them to. I have a friend who thinks that he should handle a boat hook the same way he would pull on a Tug of War rope. He gets a hold on the nearest object and puts his full weight into it. He throws off the direction and momentum of the boat so drastically that all you can do is shut down and try to finish the job manually. He means well, but does more harm than good. As captain, the control of the boat needs to be yours until you give the directive to help.

In some places, and with some boats, it is easier and preferred to pull in bow first. This tends to be easier when the current is really moving or when the wind is blowing hard. Also, it is sometimes easier for people to get off of the boat from the bow. Docking this way is an acceptable method and does not infer that you cannot do it any other way.

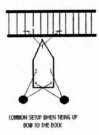

COMMON SETUP WHEN TIEING UP
BOW TO THE DOCK

It is also smart to dock bow first if the water depth at the dock is marginal. This keeps your engine or running gear in deeper water and prevents damage. A good captain is able to assess each situation and with the knowledge he has about how his boat handles and reacts, can make a decision about how best to dock his boat.

Remember, when using boat hooks, etiquette here is to grab pilings, docks, ropes etc. You should refrain from touching other boats unless you have no other choice. You surely do not want to slip and scratch someone else's gel coat or new coat of varnish. Also, use a sufficient number of fenders to protect your boat as well as your neighbors.

Once you are in, you need to tie up. Many places do not supply dock lines. Keep at least six lines on board at all times. Depending upon the size of your boat, each should be at least 25 feet of 3/8 or ½ inch material. I prefer 3 strand nylon line with a spliced eye. That means that a loop is already in one end. The loop generally goes to the dock or piling and offers you much versatility depending upon what you find to tie up to. The unlooped end is kept onboard to allow you to make final adjustments without having to get off the boat. If it is so desired, by reversing the looped end the final adjustments can be made from the dock.

Generally four lines are sufficient to keep your boat fast

to the dock. If you are tying up to a floating dock, which rises and falls with the tide, you do not need to concern yourself with making provisions for tidal changes. If you are tying up to a pier or stationary dock, you need to leave extra slack in the lines to allow your boat to move with the tide. Of course, checking the boat from time to time is necessary to make sure this all plays out as planned. When tying up stern to the dock, it is customary to run a port and starboard line called a spring line from the amidships cleat which is sometimes referred to as the spring cleat, forward to the piling or dock on the same side. Two more lines from the stern cleats should also be run aft to the dock. The forward spring lines prevent the boat from moving sternward toward the dock and the stern lines prevent the boat from moving forward. It is best to keep things simple. The only other line you may need is a breast line. This line is for convenience and runs perpendicular from a port or starboard cleat to the dock or finger dock if present. It is used in larger boats to keep the boat from moving away from the dock. For our purposes, we use it to pull the boat closer to the dock to allow our passengers to board easier.

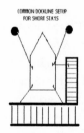

COMMON DOCKLINE SETUP
FOR SHORT STAYS

To allow for tidal changes leave as much slack in the lines as possible, but not enough to make things sloppy. If you are placing a looped line over a piling and another line is already on it, etiquette says that you should put your line through the other lines loop and over the top. This way, if the other person leaves first he can remove his line without removing yours first. Its called dipping the eye and tells the other boat owner that you know your stuff.

You may find that you need to tie up to a pier or along side a dock from time to time. Once again four lines are customary.

Common Setup When Making Fast To
A Pier

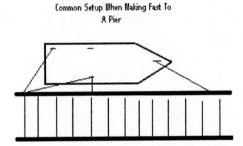

Run one bow line forward. A stern line aft. This can be from the outboard cleat to free up the inboard cleat for a spring line running from it, forward to the pier. The last line is from the spring cleat aft to the pier. A point of nomenclature is necessary here to clarify things. A line used to control forward and aft movement is called a spring line. It is named for what it does not where it attaches onboard. The spring cleat which is more correctly called an amidships cleat, may be used to attach a spring line, but also may attach a breast line. So its not always where it comes from but actually what it does that matters when naming lines.

Leaving the dock is straightforward. Board your passengers and have them sit or otherwise stay out of the way. Keep their hands in the boat and not draped over the sides where they can get injured by a passing object. Like always, start the engine before any lines are cast off. Warm up if necessary. Then, untie and stow the lines onboard or on the dock. It is preferred to coil any lines that will be left on the dock so people will not trip over them and so they can be grabbed easily when the next boat is docking. At my marina, there is one boat owner who always throws his stern lines onto the dock and leaves them wherever they land. My children invariably stumble even though I tell them to watch out for them. This creates a dangerous situation. Its not the children's fault that they trip; they are just children. It is the fault of the person that left the lines there. The fact that they are left where they are tells us a great deal about this person and his consideration for others. Keeping things shipshape is a quality that people notice and commands respect from others.

Give the directive that the last line be taken aboard. Make sure there are no lines in the water and give the throttle a little bump after making sure the coast is clear. Correct for wind and current and bump again. You are on your way, full belly and all. Find comfort in your ability to do these things properly and without incident and look forward to next time. At first they can be a challenge. Do them again and again. Practice, along with the know how, makes perfect. Albert Einstein once said, "In the midst of difficulty lies opportunity." We want the opportunity to enjoy ourselves. The difficulty we can handle with knowledge and practice. The opportunity is our reward.

Chapter 6

GETTING BACK

Heaven and hell is right now . . . You
make it heaven or you make it hell
by your actions.

—George Harrison

A hot summer's day spent on the water may be long, but usually never long enough. We usually want to eek out every possible minute, because we know that once we are back at the dock reality hits. Work, or other obligations, loom in the near future. After a fulfilling day of boating I look forward to that first person at work who asks, "How was your day off ?" "Great", I answer. What's better than that? An enjoyable day spent doing what you love with the ones you love.

As your day comes to a close, make sure that you leave enough time to get home without making it a big rush. Boating and rushing are not a good combination. Try to make the ride home just another part of the day and keep it enjoyable. Make sure that you consult the Tide Table ahead of time to

see what the state of the tide will be when you are motoring
home. You should never, ever be out on the water without
knowing at the very least, the direction the tide is moving.
Familiarize yourself with the use of a Tide Table. You may
need to add to or subtract from a particular reference location
to get the time of the tide in the area you are in. Tide tables
can be found in newspapers, books or in special computer
software. If its dead low, you may need to adjust your route
accordingly. Conversely, if its full high, you may need to
avoid low bridges or other obstacles. While we are on the
subject, bridges have a clearance measurement posted on
them somewhere.

If not, refer to your chart. It will give you a horizontal
clearance and a vertical clearance.

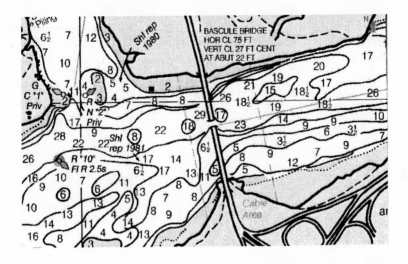

We are mostly concerned with the vertical clearance which usually corresponds to the most central sections, unless otherwise noted. This number is generally given in relation to mean high water (MHW). They want to give you the lowest height you will generally encounter. This is necessary due to the rise and fall of the tide and is given for an average high tide. This does not factor in the excessively high tides that an area may encounter due to the state of the moon or impending storms. So realize this number can and will change. If the tide is higher than average, the bridges vertical clearance is less than stated. Know your boats height including any antennas that may be projecting high up. Use this information to transit any bridges safely. Also, its good to know your areas average tidal range, which can be found on your chart.

25'

TIDAL INFORMATION

Place		Height referred to datum of soundings (MLLW)			
Name	(LAT/LONG)	Mean Higher High Water	Mean High Water	Mean Low Water	Extreme Low Water
		feet	feet	feet	feet
Fire Island Breakwater	(40°37'N/73°18'W)	4.6	4.3	0.2	-2.0
East Rockaway Inlet	(40°36'N/73°44'W)	4.6	4.3	0.2	-3.0
Governors Island	(40°42'N/74°01'W)	4.9	4.6	0.2	-4.0
Sandy Hook	(40°28'N/74°01'W)	5.2	4.9	0.2	-4.5
Asbury Park	(40°13'N/74°00'W)	4.8	4.5	0.2	-4.0

(396)Latest information available.

Copiague

Lindenhurst

AMITYVILLE

Massapequa

TANK

This is important so you can extrapolate vertical clearances at times other than high.

Remember to be aware of swells or wakes which you may encounter under the bridge. If you have three feet of clearance, but are hit with a three foot wake, well no go. I recently sat back and watched a police boat with a flying bridge pass under a bridge with a very low vertical height. The two officers had to actually duck their heads to pass through. I was amazed at the risk they were taking, but later realized it was probably done out of ignorance. They just did not recognize the danger if the boat rose even just six inches. Lets not make the same mistake.

While on the subject of bridges, keep in mind that you need to slow down to a safe speed to pass under a bridge. Bridges are generally immovable objects and can cause great damage if contacted at a high rate of speed. In my home boating territory, we have a 5 MPH speed restriction in effect when passing under a bridge. This however, at times, is too slow and can create a dangerous control problem if the current is really moving. Bridges are generally built at constrictions or narrow areas in a channel. This is done to make the bridge span as small as possible and to save money as well. These areas display what I call the Venturi Effect. Water flowing through these constrictions will increase its velocity. Therefore, expect fast moving water when transiting any bridge and keep alert to problems steering. Sometimes a little more headway is necessary to counter this effect. I am not advocating speeding, just advance the throttle enough to keep in control of your boat.

When planning your trip home, keep in mind that the end of your day may also be the end of everyone else's day. On crowded waterways, plan for a slower go home due to increased boat traffic. If you do not feel comfortable on the water at night, keep this in mind as well when planning your departure.

Some special skills are required when using the water at night. You must realize that things tend to look different at night. You may have traveled a given route hundreds of times by day, but at night, it will be more of a challenge. You need to pick your way from buoy to buoy, leaving the correct color on the proper side as you go. Buoys if lighted will always have flashing lights on them. If you see a red or green non-flashing light, it is not a buoy. Most likely this light belongs to a boat and rather than heading toward it, you should do the opposite. A searchlight, either hand held or remotely operated is a must. Proper use of your light is important to avoid affecting your vision. Make sure that you use it sparingly and do not shine it in another captains eyes or reflect it off of another boats white hull and back into your own eyes. A good lookout is mandatory when boating at night. The lookout should assist you in locating your next buoy and also look for debris in the water.

Both the captain and the lookout should avoid focusing on or looking at lights too long. This includes lights from bridges, roadways, lights on land, from other boats or cars on nearby roads. Looking at any light will adversely affect your night adjusted vision and make it more difficult to see the subtle or less well lit objects. Any cabin lights or lights on your electronics or compass should be dimmed or be red. Red lights will have a less deleterious effect on your night vision. When looking at several lights on the water, it can at times be very difficult to tell which light is closer to you, such as a light on shore verses a light on the water. An old trick used to determine where one light is in relation to another is called "Bobbing the Light". For example, if you see two lights ahead of you they may be the white anchor lights of two boats or a light from a boat and an object on shore. You look toward both and lower the height of your eyes by bending over or bending at the knees. The first one to disappear is the farthest away. This occurs because of the earths curvature and may help you out in a pinch in determining if you are looking at another boat or a distant street light. Try it next time you are out at night. You do not have to be on a boat. As long as the objects are not too close to you, it works like a charm.

Your GPS is invaluable at night as well. You must have first programmed all of your way points. Then it is just a matter of picking your way from point to point. A chart plotter is really a better choice. It receives your current position via GPS and places your vessel on an electronic chart. This is such a valuable tool to have sitting in front of you. Remember, however, that this shows you where you are and if programed properly, how to get home. It fails to tell you what is in front of you or crossing your path. Radar will tell you more about the land masses, traffic or other obstructions in your area, but is beyond the scope of this book. You still need to keep your attention on the water and keep your lookout attentive. Night vision aids, such as binoculars or monoculars are a great help. They are a costly item and probably not a practical investment for us mostly daytime pleasure boaters. It is best to assess your own risk and make your own decision.

The water at night is a wonderful place. Usually the wind lays down and the water flattens out. The best advice I can give about nighttime boating is to just do everything a little slower. Refrain from looking at bright lights. Get help from other crew members and make sure that you have plenty of water under you. Be certain to consult your tide table before you leave port and stay in the center of the channel. Furthermore, avoid boating in bad weather at night as the two are a dangerous combination even for the most seasoned boater.

Before arriving at your marina or mooring take a moment to prepare. Clear the cockpit of anything that could become a tripping hazard and place your boat hooks at the ready. Once again position your helpers and instruct them as to what to do and just as important, what not to do. Mainly, remind them to follow your instructions.

When pulling into a marina, there are a multitude of possible situations that you may encounter. Most of the time it is customary to back into your particular slip. Usually, due to the marina's layout, this must be done from one direction only. This requirement may prevent you from planning for current and wind. We know that we like to back against the current, but this may not always be possible. All of the other principles you have learned so far still apply. Go slow, bump the throttle and react to the forces that we cannot control. These are of course our foes, wind and current. Approach your slip as slowly as possible, while still maintaining steerage. Go back and forth between forward and neutral to keep your speed down. In tight quarters, most boats go too fast even at idle. Use neutral to slow your boat down. I cannot reiterate this enough. The proper use of neutral is key to going slow enough. This will allow you to dock your boat smoothly and safely. Bring your stern in as close and as perpendicular as possible to your slip and begin backing slowly. First to stop your forward motion and then to begin moving astern, look over your right shoulder and guide your boat as necessary. Direct your assistants to help when needed.

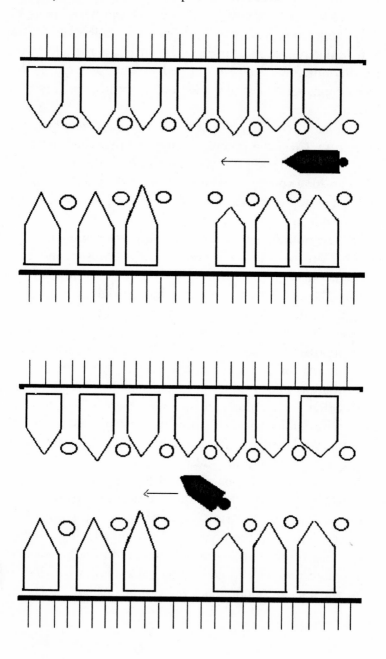

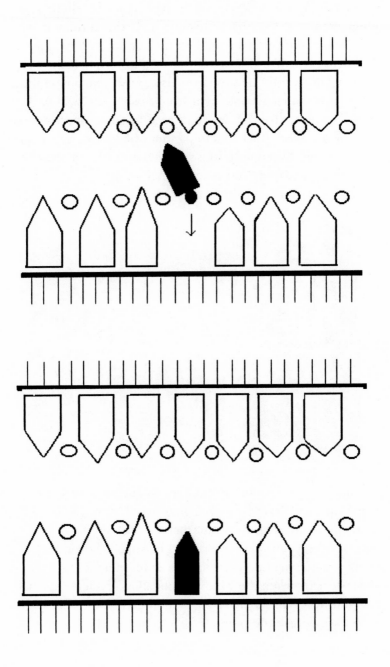

If the current is against you, pass your slip slightly and allow it to push you back towards it. If the current is with you, begin your turn early and let the current push you in the right direction. Wind may be the monkey wrench. Just stay alert and do the best that you can. Try to learn your boats special traits, such as that a single right hand screw vessel will back to port. This may save the day from time to time, especially in a tight marina where that kick to port may be just what you need to line things up properly. Most marinas are tight on space and you must watch your bow when maneuvering.

As you get into position, just before you begin to back toward your slip, your bow may get dangerously close to the boats on the opposite side. Be aware that this may limit you in your ability to get perpendicular to your slip. While not ideal, another angle may be necessary to enter your slip. I have at times, usually when the wind will not allow an ideal approach, found it necessary to lay against a piling as far aft as possible. I would then use the piling to pivot into my slip.

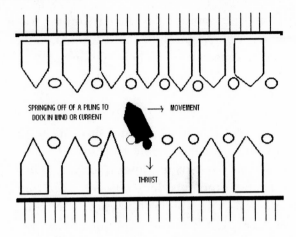

SPRINGING OFF OF A PILING TO DOCK IN WIND OR CURRENT — MOVEMENT

THRUST

It is a very effective technique when the ideal is just not possible. These are things that require foresight and preplanning. Be confident and with practice, you will get the hang of it.

I once owned a big old single screw inboard which I happened to keep in a very narrow marina. This marina was horseshoe shaped and had boats on both sides. The combination of the single screw inboard and the tight marina had all the makings for disaster. I would spend the first half of my day thrilled that I actually got out of the marina and the last half of my day worrying about backing into my slip. One day after my wife referred to me as a manic depressive, I realized that this was no way to live. I was on the water to relieve my stress and here I was creating more. I decided then and there that I would beat this fear. For a few weeks, I would head to the marina just before dusk when very few people were around. Cloudy and rainy days were even better. I would pull out, turn around and pull back in. I did this dozens of times over a few week period. It did not make me a pro but it did teach me a great deal. Mostly, about how this boat worked and just how it was affected by wind and current. It gave me confidence and I began to enjoy my days on the water again. I think the most important thing that I learned, in that period of time can be extrapolated to help me on any boat, of any size, anywhere, that is, what to do when things go bad in close quarters.

Some of this you know already or is common sense, but tend to forget in a pinch. Going slow in the first place gives you a little bit more time to think. This is critical. Additionally, pride means nothing. If anyone tells you that they never have problems docking, they are lying to you. That alone tells you about the type of person you are talking to. Everyone is in the same proverbial boat. If the marina is tight for you, then it is tight for them too. Given enough opportunity, they will have a challenge docking. So forget pride. Forget that people may be watching you and concentrate on the job at hand. Realize that the reason people are watching in the first place is to make themselves feel better about their own inadequacies. Occasionally, they may see someone who screws up worse than them. It is what I term the car race mentality. The majority of people who watch car races could care less about who wins. They watch just to see the crashes. The worse the crash, the happier they are. When someone is hurt or God forbid dies, they are ecstatic. Who needs them anyway? The best way to disappoint these gawkers is to realize that when things are not going just right, it may be time to abort your attempt. When necessary this is not only the right thing to do it is the noble thing to do. While making your approach, a wind gust may throw you off or the current may be stronger than you initially thought. You may decide to turn that approach into a U turn or a three point turn. Head on out and try again. Granted you still need to come back in and retry but, you will be armed with the additional knowledge gained by what just happened as an asset. Use this information that you just gathered, so that you do not make the same mistake twice. There is absolutely no shame in this. I will bet that those people watching will admire the guts it took to recognize when its better to just start over. Remember, a situation like this should challenge you, not sadden you. Rise to the occasion, come back in and wow them.

If the situation is not that bad, just not exactly how you want it, you can try to make some corrections. One choice is to pull ahead, correct your position and back toward your slip. This may take a couple of tries to correct for a large error. Another ace in the hole lies with your helpers. Some days, the best you will get is to come within a boat hooks length from your slip. I carry boat hooks that extend to eight feet. Give your commands. Let the helpers grab the pilings or dock and pull you in. Another choice when things go from bad to worse is to just simply shut down. You reach a point when your errors maximize and your corrections need to be made in short fast bursts. This is when people get hurt and property gets damaged. Know enough to shift to neutral, give the command to help or grab a boat hook and do it yourself. Some say that with a larger boat this is not possible. That may be true but, how big is too big?

The tight marina that I had the single screw inboard in a few years ago offers a great example. It was a 70 slip marina and every one of those boats was launched and hauled each year without ever being started up. The owner of the marina said that for insurance reasons, he was not allowed to pilot the boats from the lift to their slip or visa versa. I realized after a while, that even he knew the marina was too tight. He was afraid of embarrassment or damaging other boats; and this guy owned the place! The biggest boat they had was a whopping 35 footer. Way too big for this marina, which was probably the reason I never saw it move. They used it like a very expensive kitchen and dining room. Preparing and eating beautiful meals while in this low stress environment and always safely tied up to the dock. Anyway, the owner of the marina would launch a boat with the travel lift, hop aboard and use a boat hook to maneuver the boat down the center of the marina to it's slip. He would then, using only a boat hook, deposit it in its slip, stern first. This was done expertly in all kinds of weather. It was an art and truly an acquired skill, but it showed me that it can be done. So when the going gets tough, the boat hook is the way to go. Embarrassing, you say? No way. The end justifies the means. We want to end our day safely back at our slip. If this occurs with no injuries or damage, then we had a good day. Remember, everyone has been in those shoes. Sometimes they just need to be reminded of that. If they see you having a tough time, that should be reminder enough.

Once in, shut the engines and tie up. You tie up a bit differently than at a temporary slip. Your lines should be rigged so that it is easy to tie up the same way each time. Usually marinas want every boat tied up the same so they all tend to move in unison. Look at the way everyone else is tied up or ask in the marina office to be sure.

Common Dockline
Setup

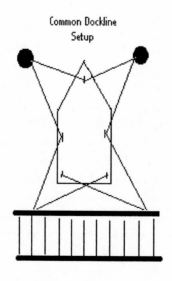

Generally, when docking stern first, a line will run up each side and be attached to the stern or amidships cleat. This line may continue traveling to a piling or other retainer. The best way to attach this line is by tying a loop at just the right spot, where the boat is kept from moving forward or backward. You then use this loop to tie off all season. Another set of lines should cross at the stern and tie off to the stern cleats. Again, loops make this reproducible each time. This set of lines prevents lateral or sideways movement at the stern. Lastly, you need this same lateral stability at the bow. So a line from a forward piling or comparable structure should be tied, both port and starboard, to a bow cleat. When using new line, make sure to readjust these lines after a few days as they will stretch. Most lines will stretch from use, especially after they get wet a few times.

If you tie up alongside a bulkhead or a dock, you need both a stern line and a bow line running perpendicular from the dock to the boat. I also suggest both a forward and aft spring line to counter movement in both of those directions. If you are not tying up to a floating dock, you also need a way to keep the boat from being damaged by tidal movements or waves. Fenders are essential and you should use several. Products like Mooring Whips are great as they keep the boat away from the bulkhead or dock. There are many options available to accomplish this goal. They include, drive on docking systems or the creme de la creme, a hoist. Hoists, lift your boat entirely out of the water, keeping it safe from tides, waves, barnacles etc. etc. etc. Check out the marine supply store for ideas that fit your application.

Lastly, some people keep their boat on a mooring. A mooring is, a firmly anchored chain or chain and nylon line with an attached float which is placed away from the shore in deep water. The anchoring device is usually a large piece of concrete or a large mushroom anchor.

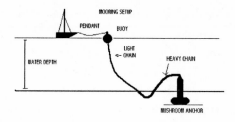

To pick up your mooring you should try to approach against the current. We will assume for now that because of waters density, that water will have a greater effect upon your boat than wind. On some days however, this may not be true. Have a person stationed at the bow to direct you and to use a boat hook to pick up the mooring line from the buoy. More correctly, the line from the mooring which attaches the vessel to the mooring is called the Pendant. This is generally a nylon line. As you get close to your mooring, you will most likely lose sight of the buoy. This is when communication is essential. If you are alone, try to bring the buoy alongside and grab it with the hook. You may need to pass it and drift back until it is close enough to grab.

With all lines, but with the mooring lines especially, some type of chaffing gear is essential. With the constant movement of the boat on a mooring, anywhere the line touches another object, such as the boat, the line is subject to wear and can fail at that location.

Chaffing gear is a canvas or rubber sleeve which goes over the line to prevent this wear. Any line which is stressed and under continual movement needs some type of chaffing gear to protect it.

While I am well aware that there is an infinite number of docking configurations, approaches and marina designs. As well as, docks that rise and fall with the tide and those that do not. I cannot describe every possible situation to you. It is the general principles that I have tried to get across. With the ultimate advice being, practice makes perfect. You will not improve and build your confidence if you do not get out there and do it. Try hard to do the best you can and do not be afraid to stop when you are in a jam. Tie your boat up well and head home with the knowledge that you did the best you could and returned home safely. Most importantly, do not get intimidated. A boat is just a mechanical device. Handling it is nothing more than a challenge that we need to address and conquer. With knowledge and self confidence this can definitely be achieved.

Chapter 7

MARLINESPIKE SEAMANSHIP

Skill to do comes of doing.
—Ralph Waldo Emerson

Marlinespike Seamanship is the overall knowledge of knots and the general care of rope. A Marlinespike or Fid, is a long slender tool used to separate the strands of a rope to aid in splicing. It is an ancient term where a Marline was a small diameter line used for various purposes aboard vessels many centuries ago. It is believed that the Billfish or Marlin derived its name from the Marlinespike, aptly named for its spear like protuberance.

Beginning with nomenclature, a rope is what you buy in a store, as soon as it is brought onboard a boat it is called a line. A knowledgeable boater never uses the word rope onboard. The Standing Part of the line is the long end. The other end is called the Bitter End. A turn or U shape in the standing part is called a Bight and a small circle in the line is a Loop. A Splice is used to join two lines together and an Eye Splice makes a permanent loop in a line.

Whipping is the finishing of the end of a line, so that it does not fray and become unsightly. A line may be whipped by melting the end of a synthetic line, by wrapping it with waterproof tape, by using a heat shrink tube, by dipping the end in a liquid plastic or by using thread to sew the end tight.

While there are over 3000 different knots, a boater can get away with proficiency in a few. You most definitely need to know how to make a line fast to a cleat. Only one turn around the base is necessary and then a figure eight will do. If you are leaving the boat unattended, then a half hitch over one horn of the cleat will give you extra security.

A Clove Hitch is used to fasten a line to a piling or to attach a fender to a rail.

It unties easily when not under tension, but can be quite difficult to untie when you are unable to relieve the tension on it. For this reason, when tying off to a piling, I prefer to use a line with a loop in the end formed with an eye splice. Just placing the eye around the piling is easy enough and you never have to worry about tension. The only problem that you may encounter, is if the piling is excessively high or excessively wide. Therefore, a Clove Hitch is a knot that you should know if you need to use it in a pinch.

Next is the Bowline.

It is probably the most used, most versatile knot to know. If you do not know any other knot, you must know the Bowline. It became famous in the original Jaws movie, during that great scene in the boat's cabin. Quint is teaching the knot to Chief Browdy. In his salty, gruff voice he says, "the rabbit comes out of the hole, goes around the tree and goes back into the hole". Well, you get the picture. He is referring to the ropes bitter end and how it should be wrapped around the standing part of the line. A Bowline is used to form a fixed loop in a line which is temporary in nature. That is, by pushing on the small bight in the standing part of the line, you can easily untie it, even after it has come under great tension. You can use it to tie dock lines to deck fittings. It can be used to attach two lines together, even if they are of unequal size. Practice this knot, it is a must know for every boater.

The Fisherman's Bend is also a good simple knot to know for attaching a line to an object.

It is a strong knot, but it may be impossible to untie after it comes under tension. It is generally used for a fairly permanent situation. For example, when tying a line to an anchor fitting. For a less permanent solution, a Bowline could be used in place of the Fisherman's Bend.

Some general information about lines is important because

lines need to be sized properly to do the job asked of them. For our applications, small boats used in inshore locations, 3/8 inch line is frequently used. I however prefer ½ inch line for all boats over 18 feet, especially for anchor line. Make sure that ½ inch line will not bog down on your deck cleats and prevent you from tying a good knot that will not slip. Some manufacturers supply very small cleats, making your only option 3/8 inch line. We should all be using synthetic lines for their resistance to chafe, oil, grease, gasoline and UV rays. Additionally, they stretch and offer a great ability to absorb the energy from sudden shocks caused by wakes or collisions. They also do not rot or mildew and can be stowed wet.

Three strand nylon line is relatively inexpensive. It can be used for all situations that we may encounter. It can be purchased pre washed and pre shrunk. It also can be coated with a marine finish, which can offer greater abrasion resistance and the line should therefore last longer under most situations. Look for the premium line when you are buying, it will better serve you.

Braided line or Double Braid as it is usually called, is essentially two lines in one. It has a braided inner core and a braided outer core for strength. Double Braid is generally stronger, more flexible and easier on the hands than Three Strand. Buy what you can afford. The premium Three Strand is probably better than the cheapest Double Braid. Consider the intended use, the load it will be under and the chafe it will encounter. Remember, that ½ inch thick line may be the only thing between your boat and the rocks. Use what you feel comfortable with.

Care of your lines is important as it will extend their life. All lines will benefit from a cleaning in fresh water once in a while. You can wash them in a washing machine by placing them in a mesh bag or a pillow case. This prevents the line from wrapping itself around the inside of your washing machine and rendering it forever useless. A little fabric softener will make them easier to work with. Remove any kinks or twists often and always coil your lines for storage.

Three strand is coiled by looping an arms length at a time. Only a neophyte coils line by wrapping it from your thumb to your elbow. That method tends to put twists into the line. Double Braid never coils, rather it forms a figure eight when you loop it upon itself. Once in a while, you should reverse a line end for end to extend it's life. This wears the line in different locations instead of always in the same areas. Always use chafing gear, as discussed earlier to minimize the effects of abrasion in specific spots. Chafing gear should be used anywhere that the standing part of the line comes in contact with anything. The constant movement of the boat can cause quite a bit of wear and tear on a line. It is better to wear your chafing gear than your line.

Polypropylene line is also a synthetic line. It is not as strong as nylon and suffers greatly from exposure to UV rays. The one great advantage of this line is that it floats. It is therefore commonly used for ski rope and tow lines for tubes and dinghies. The fact that it floats helps to keep it away from the boats prop. It should never be used as dock line as it will breakdown quickly from exposure to the sun and some knots will slip if they are not tied very tight.

Keep extra line onboard for whatever purpose you feel you may need it for. A recent experience that I had drives this point home. I was onboard a friends boat, fishing in the Atlantic Ocean in about 70 feet of water. This depth is found about two miles offshore. After a long drift we went to restart, only to find the outboard uncooperative. It seemed fuel starved and we quickly came up with several possibilities. When it became apparent that this could take quite some time, I suggested dropping the anchor. At this depth, to hold bottom we would need to pay out quite a bit of rode. For a minimal scope of 7:1, you would need at least 490 feet of rode in 70 feet of water. Realizing that the wind, coupled with an incoming tide was pushing us shoreward at a rate of 2 knots, I quickly calculated that it would be only one hour before we were in the breakers at the beach. Now this fellow, who I felt was a knowledgeable, savvy skipper told me that he had only 150 feet of rode on his primary anchor. At this rate of drift we would be lucky if this anchor even touched bottom. I asked him where his extra line was and he went pale. His secondary anchor had 100 feet of rode. Tying the two together would give us 250 feet of line, giving us a scope of about 3.5:1. With this fast drift and the 3 foot ground swells, we would never hold bottom. It was not even worth spending the time trying.

Fortunately, within 20 minutes we had the problem corrected and we were on our way home. Interestingly, the problem was found to be a loss of prime or the inability of the fuel pump to bring gas to the engine, caused by an air leak in the fuel line. The manufacturer used cheap plastic cable ties to clamp the fuel lines at their connections, rather than stainless steel hose clamps. We were able to temporarily override the problem by pumping the primer ball whenever the engine began to stall. We lost time diagnosing the problem because we erroneously thought the problem to be a clogged fuel filter. We thought that the rough ocean run to where we were fishing had dislodged sludge and sediment in the fuel tank and clogged the filter. We did have a spare fuel filter, but under the conditions, it would have taken us quite a few more minutes to do the job, way too close for comfort for me.

Later that day at the marine store, my friend purchased two spools of 200 feet, ½ inch, three strand nylon line. They will be coiled and will stay on board forever. If he ever intends to venture into deeper water he will buy a third or fourth spool. Incidentally, that bowline that you learned to tie would be a good knot to use to attach these lines together. You could also splice in an eye loop with a metal thimble into each end of the line and then use a quick link or similar device to connect them. The point here, once again, is to think things through before you leave the dock. When things go bad, they tend to do so quickly. You need to be prepared for the worst.

Just for kicks, lets discuss some other options that you would have had in the above situation, if you were not able to correct the problem right away. First, you would call your commercial towing company on VHF channel 16. Ask for a tow and ascertain the boats estimated time of arrival. Ask the Captain to keep you advised of his progress on the working channel that he suggests, not on channel 16. You may want to advise the nearest Coast Guard Station of your situation. They will establish a schedule of contact with you to keep them on top of your situation. Usually, they will contact you every fifteen minutes until you are no longer at risk. You could ask any boats in your vicinity to take you in tow to keep you in safe waters until your commercial tower arrives. Also, remember that as you get closer to shore the water depth will decrease and your anchor may then be able to hold bottom. Almost always you will have options, think them through and do what you have to.

Marlinspike Seamanship is important. It is necessary to use good lines and good knots. The knots that you use must be appropriate for the job at hand and practiced in advance so they can be done expeditiously and with minimal thought. You have a great deal riding on them.

Chapter 8

Courtesy Afloat

*The entire population of the universe, with
one trifling exception, is composed of others*
—John Andrew Holmes

W hen I first started boating many years ago at age 5,
there were no commercial towers in operation.

The Coast Guard was available to tow, but only if you were in danger and definitely only to the nearest port. They were over worked and under staffed even then. Towing a disabled boat was everyone's responsibility and was considered a common courtesy. All you needed to do was to take the engine cover off and people from all around would ask if you needed help. While they were lending a hand, other boaters passing by would slow down so as not to "wake" you in your time of need. Towing you and your disabled boat was an act of kindness and rarely would the tower take even as much as gas money for his efforts. He may be in a similar situation someday and appreciate the same courtesy.

Well, we know that things have changed quite a bit from those days. The waters have gotten crowded and people feel that they do not need to help out because the guy behind them probably will. For every situation you see unfolding out there, picture yourself or your loved ones in it. Never assume that help is on the way or that the guy behind you will stop and help. A quick shout offering assistance makes people feel better and means a lot. If they take you up on your offer, all the better. You always feel good when you help out someone in need. Even if it is just placing a phone call for them, staying with them until their tow arrives or going the distance and towing them back to port. Whatever assistance you render is a great service and something you should be proud of.

When towing another vessel keep several general principles in mind. First and foremost weather is a very important consideration. If conditions are poor you may need to defer a lengthy tow to a professional. Also, the size of the vessel you need to tow may be a concern. If it is very large, you may opt to just stand by or tow it only a short distance to a safer location or less trafficked area. If you do make the decision to tow the disabled vessel, a little pre planning will help a lot.

I have pre rigged a special line and a bridle and have it stowed in an easily accessible, but out of the way location. The tow line consists of a double braided nylon line about 75 feet long. I prefer braided line in a towing situation because it is less elastic than three stranded nylon and will be less apt to snap back if something breaks. I purchase it with a loop spliced in one end. Through this loop I pass the bridle. A bridle is a shorter line of the same material, which I attach to both the port and starboard stern cleats. Some boats have well placed U bolts attached to the transom. These can be used as well as a point of attachment of the bridle. Snap hooks placed in the bridle ahead of time will make setting up this system very simple. A bridle offers you much better handling when towing. Many times people suggest attaching the line to the towing vessel as far forward as possible to increase maneuverability. In our situations, a pleasure craft towing a pleasure craft, this is not usually practical and may be unsafe. If a line parts or a cleat separates, I feel it is best to have this line away from the most likely spot passengers may be. In my experience, I feel you have little to gain in maneuverability and a lot to lose if a problem arises.

Attaching the towing line to the disabled vessel is simple. Use the bow eye if possible or else use the forward cleat. Tie off the bitter end if this line somewhere else on board, such as the amidships cleat to prevent a dangerous spring back if the bow cleat fails. Slowly and gradually begin to move. Try not to be too aggressive or go to fast. The amount of line you need to let out is different for every situation. A general rule of thumb is; more line for rougher conditions and faster towing, less line for more control on calmer days and when going slower. If you are towing a bit faster, try to adjust the lines to keep the towed boat in step. This means that both boats should be taking the waves the same way, both on the crest or both in the trough, if this is not possible then slow down. One last note is to always keep a means of releasing the tow line handy. If things go bad, part the line. This is best accomplished with a knife.

Courtesy on the water can take on many other forms and is regarded as a sign of good seamanship. It can be as simple as putting out extra fenders on a windy day to protect the boat tied up next to yours. Similarly, it can take the form of you trying to contact a boater by VHF radio to tell them that they have strayed into an area of low water and are at risk of grounding. Slowing down to decrease your wake in an area where boats are anchored or are fishing may not always be possible, but is a nice gesture as well. Of course, it should not be necessary to remind people to observe the posted speed limits.

They are in place for a reason. I commonly see people speeding through areas posted at 5 MPH, but they intentionally stay just outside of the markers, in the flats, to technically avoid breaking the law. What they may not be realizing is the reason for the speed restriction in the first place. It may be there to protect the docks and bulkheading of waterfront homes in the area from constant wave action. Sometimes the reason for the speed limit is not that apparent. In some cases it may be in place to reduce bank erosion and thereby not wipe out the natural habitat of certain animals. By blowing by, twenty feet from the channel you may have avoided the legal issue but still have had an ill effect on the area.

There is a growing list of issues regarding Personal Water Craft (PWC). Many people feel they are a nuisance and are too dangerous. Age restrictions, Safe Boating Class requirements and speed controls which limit top end speed have helped the situation. Also, law enforcement has done wonders and is certainly responsible for preventing many accidents. I feel however, that things need to be taken further to ensure a peaceful coexistence. Some type of waterproof helmet should be required. Head injuries, just like on motorcycles, are an ever present threat. In addition, identifying numbers should be displayed on the craft and maybe even on the life vest of the operator. This will help in identifying those engaged in unlawful conduct.

I was once witness to a group of six PWC riders jumping wakes around a 40 foot vessel. They were jumping both the bow and stern wakes creating a very dangerous situation. The vessels captain would lose sight of those riders under his bow and was afraid to slow down for fear that those behind would not realize he was slowing and crash into his stern. The frightened captain alerted the Coast Guard, who responded very quickly. By the time they were on scene, however, the PWC were gone. The captain was unable to identify the offenders because they really do all look alike. If they were more easily identifiable and knew it, they might be less apt to engage in dangerous behavior.

Please do not misinterpret this suggestion, most PWC operators are responsible, law abiding captains who enjoy their sport safely and in a respectful manner. Just because you own a PWC does not make you a bad person. As with other things in life, 10% of the people cause 90% of the problems. This 10% however, influences the public's perception of the sport as a whole. I guess the real issue is your impact on others. Whether you operate a PWC or a 50 foot yacht, if your noisy and invade others space, then you are not being courteous. Do your best to think of how your actions may be affecting the person closest to you. If you feel that you are bothering others, than do it differently or do it elsewhere.

There was a very corny ad campaign once, that never really caught on, but had great meaning. It took the form of a bunch of billboards placed along several expressways. They said very simply, Courtesy is Contagious. The theory here is that if you are nice to someone, they will be happy about it and in turn be nice to someone else. That wave of your hand that you flash to a passing boater turns into a few more waves by that boater and sooner or later everyone is waving to everyone else. Just as it should be. It gives you a sense of friendship and comradery and makes it more difficult to hit the throttle and wake the guy and his family that just waved a nice hello to you. This is where it begins. Start small and start waving. Over time this will give boating the good name it deserves. You might just find, that wave comes back to you in good ways, many times over.

Chapter 9

TRAILERING

Nothing is particularly hard if
you divide it into small jobs.

—*Henry Ford*

Trailering a boat is a perfect choice for some boaters, while others would not even consider it as an option. First of all, not every boat is trailering material. Generally, any boat beamier than 8 ½ feet is considered a wide load over land, and therefore, not intended for routine trailering. Length is more negotiable, but when you start getting up in size, my personal opinion is that some boats just belong floating in the water and not on a trailer at all. Weight is an issue as well and your tow vehicle must be rated to carry the gross weight of the vessel. This includes not only the hull and engines, but all of the gear and fuel aboard.

The advantages of trailering are many and include much more than the cost savings you enjoy by keeping your boat at home, rather than in a marina. One of the biggest advantages is peace of mind. When that hurricane is barreling up the coast, you will feel secure in knowing that your boat is on dry land, or better yet, in your garage. Damage can certainly still occur on land, but at least the odds may be a bit more in your favor. I also like the idea that you can access a greater area in a shorter period of time. What I mean is that you have more choices of where you can put in. I live on Long Island and use my boat most of the time on the South Shore. I do, however, have the option of trailering up to the North Shore to enjoy the Long Island Sound, even the Peconic Bay or Montauk Point. I do this regularly and probably would never boat in these areas if I had to get to them by water. Also, as I have mentioned previously, I am not afraid to hit the Chesapeake Bay several times a year, an option that would be out of the question for me, by water. Every year I explore more areas and get to new places because of the versatility of having a trailerable rig. Finally, every boat that I have kept on a trailer, at my home, has truly been in the best shape possible. Being the ultimate tinkerer, when the boat is home, I am always fixing this or adding that. It is a part of boating that I just love and having this available to me in my driveway is a bonus.

Of course there are disadvantages to trailering a boat. The inability to be very spontaneous was always a big complaint for me. When the boat has to be hooked up, driven to and dropped in, you just need that much more time in the day. When the boat is kept in the water, as long as it is close by, it just seems quicker and easier to use it, even though it may not actually be. Also, a certain amount of expertise is required to handle the boat on the trailer. I will cover this in greater depth later, but just remember a certain amount of practice is required to launch a boat from its trailer. The trailer is an additional piece of gear and therefore requires maintenance of its own. This is a whole other topic which we also cover later. Lastly, you will need a vehicle capable of doing the job and expect that vehicle to require additional maintenance as well, because it will be working harder. These things aside, if trailering your boat is what allows you to get out on the water, then do it. It is not that big a deal, once you get used to it.

There are probably more funny stories relating to trailering than any other aspect of boating. The launching ramp near my house has become a haven for people to gather, especially on the weekends when the ramp is very crowded. They sit and watch the boats being launched like it is a new spectator sport. Once again, it is that car race mentality. These people are only there to witness the problems that people may encounter. You must not let these people intimidate you. If they had any self confidence and expertise themselves, they would not be only observers, they would be participants. My favorite story most likely never occurred at all. I am sure that it is nothing more than a fabrication, but it is funny never the less. It involves a novice boater who pulls up to a fuel dock to ask for help. His new boat will not plane, is unresponsive to both steering and throttle and is generally operating miserably. The attendant checks a few things at the engine, which seems to all be in order. Confused, he decides to dive under the boat to check things out. To his surprise he finds the trailer still attached to the boat. Of course, we can pick this story apart and realize its shortcomings. There are a million more stories which are most likely true and involve premature launchings while still on the ramp or better yet launching the boat, trailer and tow vehicle all at once. Let's go through the proper techniques so you will not become yet another story.

First, make sure the trailer fits the boat. Either the boat dealer will sell the proper trailer with the boat or you should go to a reputable trailer dealer and have them match one up for you. If you buy a used boat and trailer, do not assume that they are matched. Have it checked out. There are as many types of trailers as there are types of boats out there. Ask the pro's for advice regarding both the type of trailer you are using and the way your boat is set on the trailer. One important consideration here is tongue weight. It is the weight of the trailers tongue as it sits on the hitch. Ideally, it should be between 5-10% of the overall weight you are pulling. That is the weight of the trailer, boat, fuel and whatever else you are carrying in the boat. If the tongue weight is too light, the trailer will tend to sway from side to side or even surge forward or back while being pulled. If it is too heavy, it may be hard to handle the tow vehicle, strain the suspension of the vehicle and cause the rear tires to wear prematurely. A good trailer shop should be able to measure this weight and adjust it if necessary. Adjustments are made by moving the boat forward or backward on the trailer. Also, make sure the boat is well supported on the trailer. If and when you encounter rough roads, the impact must be dispersed properly over as large a section of the hull as possible. Failure to do this can cause severe structural problems to the hull resulting in a costly repair.

Make sure that you always use a good quality transom strap to make fast the rear of the boat with the trailer.

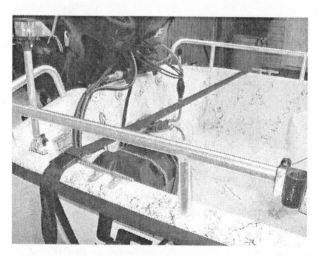

The type that have some sort of winching mechanism to allow

you to sufficiently tighten the strap is preferred. Most trailers provide hooks or holes for the straps to attach. This allows the boat and the trailer to move as one unit, taking advantage of the trailers springs to absorb most of the pounding the road has to offer. Additionally, outboards and I/O's should always be tilted up as far as possible to avoid hitting the lower unit on the roadway. To take the stress off of the boats transom, a motor support should be used.

This is an inexpensive device that attaches to the trailer and rests against the lower unit of the engine or drive. It supports the engine and also transfers any stresses from the road to the trailer instead of through the transom, where it could eventually do damage. It is a must, even if you only trailer a short distance. Many outboards have a brace that folds down from under the engine's cowling and fits into the mounting bracket. This is designed to protect the engines hydraulic system but is in no way a replacement for a motor support. It does nothing to protect the transom, which is really very important.

Another piece of safety equipment is your winch strap or cable.

It holds the boat via the bow eye to the trailer via the winch. Make sure the cable or strap is in good condition and not corroding or fraying. A chain should always be used as a precaution. It should be permanently attached to the winch post and be hooked onto the bow eye each time you bring the boat up. These items act separately to keep your boat on the trailer at all times and allow it to safely take all the abuse the road has to offer.

The connection of the trailer to the tow vehicle is also critical. Use only the proper size ball for the trailer's coupler, usually 1 7/8" or 2". They are not interchangeable. You may say; "What's the big deal? its only 1/8". It is a big deal. Chances are, if your trailer detaches from your vehicle you may not be in great danger, but someone around you will be. I have never personally witnessed a boat and trailer traveling down the highway at great speeds and out of control. I have however, heard stories and have been told it is one of the most frightening sights you may ever see. Both the coupler and ball are stamped with their size.

Make sure that you have a match.

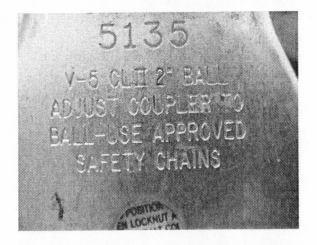

Additionally, safety chains need to be attached between the trailer and tow vehicle. All hitches have a place for them. Make sure that you cross them under the trailers tongue when you attach them. They keep your trailer attached to your vehicle should the worst happen.

Lastly, the lights need to be connected and checked to confirm that they are operating properly. All states require that trailers be equipped with signal, safety and stop lights which are operated by the driver. Generally, the 80" rule applies in just about all states. It says that trailers, under 80" in width need red reflector lights at the trailers back, combining all of the required lights. In addition, a white license plate light and a yellow marker light on each side are needed. Trailers over 80" in width need to add a group of three red lights along the rear frame called identification lights and two larger combination lamps that have a minimum luminous lense area of 11.625". You also need two amber lights, called clearance lights, on the front of each fender as well as the side marker lights and license plate light. I realize this is confusing. You only need to know that wider trailers require more and larger lights. At the stores, they are labeled "over 80" lights. I bring it up so that you get what you need and stay legal.

Trailer lighting is probably the most frustrating part of the required equipment. They tend to work one day and not the next and basically have a mind of their own. This is a function of the harsh environment they encounter. There are two types of lights available for trailers today. Waterproof or submersible lights may give you less trouble, but are more expensive. Nonsubmersible lights are their less expensive equivalents, but as the name implies, they should not go underwater. They are intended for mounting above the waterline. Be careful of what you buy and try not to be fooled. Some people feel that the problem with trailer lights is entirely from their frequent immersion in salt water. I believe this to be the main culprit, but also feel that dipping a hot bulb into cool water on a regular basis does not help either. LED lights are hitting the market and are becoming standard equipment on new trailers. They boast long life and a greater resistance to the effects of the elements. They seem like a great advancement in trailer lighting but with all of the older trailers around, it will be years before our lighting troubles will be over.

In my experience, both the lights and tires need to be submerged in the water to some degree to both load and unload the boat. Many people believe that this should never be done. That dunking the lights and tires in salt water will lead to their imminent failure. I have yet to find a way to properly load and unload a boat without getting both of these trailer parts wet. In fact, most trailer manufacturers agree that at least some of the tires be submerged. We therefore need to pay particular attention to the proper care and preventive maintenance to help avoid failure of these critical systems.

A check of the lights each time you hook the trailer up is a necessity. Have a helper stand behind the trailer and check that the lights are operating properly. Check the brake lights, turn signals, headlights and flashers. The headlights light up both the red brake lights and the side marker lights which are usually amber in color. When alone, I walk back and forth to check the operation of each light. It is very important. Try to remember back to the last time you may have been following a car with its brake lights out. Its very easy to rear end a car or trailer like that. Just think of the incredible damage that can occur to your boat if it were to be rear ended by a car. Lets just say it would put an early end to your season.

Twice a year, I remove the lense covers from the lense housing and spray a water displacer and metal protectant product like WD-40 or CRC 6-56 on all connections and bulb holders. White Vinegar is good at removing existing corrosion from copper terminals, as is fine sandpaper or steel or brass wool. I also carry a complete rewiring kit for my trailer. It is inexpensive and saves a lot of time if you experience a failure while on the road. It is easier and faster to replace the entire fixture if you cannot get the old one working quickly. Later, I can clean up the bad fixture in the workshop, at my convenience, rather than in some parking lot in the dark. Of course, the proper tools for the job make life a lot easier. A good light is key. Something that can stand on its own and be directed where you are working is great. The right screwdrivers and a nut driver in the correct size is a godsend when you need it. Spare screws and nuts are great to have, as many a part is lost to the darkness in these situations. Of course, spare bulbs are a must and the first thing to try when a light fails. I keep all of this equipment in the tow vehicle in a canvas bag. The tools and extra items fit great in a plastic tackle box insert. After you have experienced the headache of lighting failures, you may look for alternate ways of mounting your lights to prevent the effects of saltwater in the first place. Many people use a pair of trailer guide ons. A somewhat vertical strut mounted on each side of the trailer that helps to position the boat properly as you winch it up. A great tool for those who boat alone. It really makes loading your boat simple, even with a stiff wind. They also serve an important secondary role, which is to act as a platform to mount your lights on, so they will never get wet again. Thus minimizing the potential problems you will experience.

One last item about lights is, that if they seem to start doing funny things like your turn signal goes out when you step on the brakes, you may have a bad ground. Some trailers are grounded through the ball, which requires that the connection of the ball to the coupler be metal to metal. Rust buildup is the usual culprit when this connection is lost. When things start acting funny, disconnect, clean and grease the ball and retry. This usually happens after the ball has not been used for a while. It is the kind of problem that causes you to pull your hair out. Take a step back and think about what is going on. It will usually begin to make sense

It is also very helpful to familiarize yourself with the use of a 12 volt tester. It looks like an ice pick with a wire and an alligator clip attached.

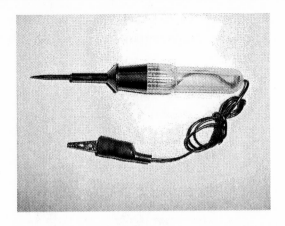

The alligator clip gets connected to a good ground. This can be any bare metal on the trailer. On a galvanized trailer, any metal will do. On a painted trailer, you need to find a part that is not painted. A bolt will usually do fine. The pointy or probe end gets pushed through the wires insulation, placed on the bare metal of a wire connector or touched around the bulbs socket. Turn on the power to the light you are testing and if the bulb in the tester's handle lights, then the problem lies elsewhere in the system, such as the fixture or the bulb. Move down the line, proceeding further from the tow vehicle until you find the problem. The fixture itself can also be tested in the same manner. Keep in mind that the best way to understand how this tool works is not with a system which has already failed, but with one which is working properly. Attach your ground and use your probe to touch various areas and see what happens. Do this with your turn signals, flashers, brakes and headlights on to see all the variations.

So, now your boat is on the proper trailer, secured well and the lights are working as they should. All that is left is to start up your tow vehicle and go. Well, you should know by now that this book is about preparing yourself for all potential complications that may arise. Realizing that, there is yet another weak link in our system. It involves the trailers tires, hubs and braking system. Rarely do trailers come with a spare tire, yet they are vitally important.

Make sure you purchase a spare tire and rim and either keep it in the tow vehicle or better yet mount it directly to the trailer. This can be accomplished using any of the after market mounting products available. If theft is an issue in your area you can get a lock for the spare tire as well. Just having a spare tire however, may not be enough. Rarely does the lug wrench you carry for your vehicle fit your trailer's lug nuts or bolts. You need to carry the correct one with you. I bought an old fashioned four size cross shaped wrench that I leave in my tow vehicle. Trailer lug nuts and bolts sometimes require a great deal of leverage to remove them as they are submerged frequently and corrode easily. The cross type lug wrench gives you the force you need to break them free.

In addition, a precaution you need to take to keep them from seizing is to remove the lug nuts or bolts when the trailer is new or newly acquired and apply Anti Seize Lubricant to the threads and then replace them. This should then be redone yearly. For the first few trips, after doing this, I check to make sure the lug nuts or bolts have not loosened or backed out a bit after they have a few miles on them. It is best to check by trying to tighten them with your lug wrench, just looking may not be enough. If you hear stories about people breaking off lugs while trying to remove them, you can bet they missed this vital precaution. Lastly, make sure you can jack up the trailer. Do not assume that your car jack will work. I carry a small pump jack and a block of wood. The wood, when placed under the jack, prevents the jack from sinking into soft ground. Bear in mind these things never need to be done under ideal circumstances.

The trailer's hubs also require regular maintenance. The hub is the collective term for the assembly which attaches the wheel to the axle and allows it to turn. The bearings which are located in the hub reduce friction and allow the wheel to spin efficiently. To do this they must be rust and corrosion free and lubricated properly. Each time you submerge the hubs, which are usually hot from the drive to the boat ramp, they are cooled quickly in the colder water and moisture is absorbed through their seals. The bearings eventually rust and the next time you use the trailer, excessive heat builds up. This is caused by the bearings operating inefficiently and can cause them to fail. In extreme cases, there can also be damage to the axle and wheel. This entire problem can be avoided most of the time by the use of bearing protectors. They are commonly referred to as bearing buddies.

They are devices that snap on in place of the bearing's dust cap. They have a grease fitting which allows them to be filled up with marine grade grease. It is spring loaded and keeps the bearings constantly greased. By doing so, moisture is unable to be absorbed and the bearings stay clean and corrosion free. You need to regularly check to make sure the bearing protectors remain full of grease. Make sure that you do not over fill them however, a little is good, a lot is not always better. Newer models have a pressure relief opening to prevent over filling and possible damage to the seals. Older models do not have this relief opening so make sure you follow the manufacturers instructions. You do not want to fill them until grease is squishing out all over the place or you can risk blowing out the seals. Stop well short of this.

Even with these precautions, have the hubs checked by a professional after every 1000 miles of use. This is a general guideline, as some people may only need to travel one mile to the ramp and never put 1000 miles on the trailer in a lifetime of use. Others, like myself, may put 1000 miles on the trailer in a month. Use your judgement and service them when you feel it is necessary. If you have some mechanical know how, carry a spare set of bearings and seals with you. Just about any mechanic can do a bearing job for you. It may however take days to get the correct parts. Carrying them with you will avoid having to wait for a delivery. Better yet, you can carry the entire hub assembly, preassembled for you ahead of time. These are available from many marine supply stores. This may very well save you some time, but requires the know how to do the job correctly. Fortunately, I have never had to do the job alone. I do, however, carry a spare hub assembly with me. I make it a point to watch the mechanic service the hubs whenever I have it done. They generally do not mind because they realize that this is sometimes necessary to be done as an emergency repair on the road. Also, ask them about any special tools that may be required to do the job. They may include a wire cutter to remove the cotter pin and a pair of Channel Lock Pliers or a water pump wrench to remove the axle nut which holds the hub assembly onto the axle. For piece of mind, one of the best values in boating, as mentioned previously, is a membership in Boat/US. For a nominal charge, of about ten dollars, you can join their trailering club. This membership includes $150.00 toward on the road repairs or towing. The best part of this membership, not including the very informative magazine you receive, is access to their 24 hour toll free dispatch line. Wherever you are, Boat/US will get assistance to you. No need to find a phone book and look up someone. It is all done for you. Most importantly, if it is run and sponsored by Boat/US you can bet that it is run superbly and that they stand by their members 100%. Its foolish to operate a boat in this country without being a member.

The final parts of your trailer's wheel assembly that we will discuss are the brakes. Every state has different laws governing trailer braking systems. In a nutshell, lighter loads, classified as rigs under 1000 pounds, do not require a separate braking system. All heavier loads do. There are two types of braking systems available, electric or surge. Electric brakes operate whenever the tow vehicles brakes are operating. Surge brakes operate when they sense the forward motion of the trailer decreasing. This is accomplished by use of a special coupler or the part of the trailer that fits over the ball. It is this coupler which senses the decrease in the trailers forward motion and applies the brakes. Surge brakes are generally hydraulically operated and work independently of the tow vehicles systems. Most newer trailers are equipped with surge brakes. Both ultimately do the same job. Due to the varying laws from state to state, trailer manufacturers are still supplying trailers with both types. Some uniformity is necessary to keep the trailer owners compliant in each state. The important thing to remember, regardless of type, is that brakes that are dipped in water regularly will need maintenance. This is definitely not a do it yourself job, unless you are a qualified mechanic. Get acquainted with a good trailer mechanic in your area and find comfort in his expertise when you hit the road.

So now you are ready to hit the ramp. Begin by backing up your vehicle to the trailer. You need to line up the vehicles tow ball with the coupler on the trailer. There are many gizmos available that help you to line things up properly including a 12 volt video camera system. I prefer to use my wife. She motions to me and we get things set up pretty well. Make sure that the trailer coupler is jacked up higher than the ball on your vehicle. When they are directly over and under one another, drop the coupler onto the ball, making sure that it seats all the way. Slide the lever down all the way to its fully locked position and put either a hitch pin or a lock through the hole. That is critical as it will prevent the lever from jumping up unexpectedly. Attach your safety chains in a cross under the coupler and onto the hitch. Connect the lights and check to make sure they are working.

Secure the transom tie down straps. Make sure the safety chain from the winch post is through the bow eye on the boat. If necessary, raise the outboard or outdrive and install the motor support. Make sure everything in the boat is secured. A bucket flying out of your boat at 55 MPH could easily kill someone in the car behind you. Yes, you are now ready to go.

Remember when driving, turns need to be made wider than usual and generally travel should be slower than if you were not trailering. Use your side view mirrors to watch your trailer clear any obstructions such as poles, curbs or people as you negotiate turns. Do not forget the extra length behind you when passing other cars and try to stop gradually rather than abruptly. When trailering anything behind you, it is best to become a follower rather than a leader. Aggressive driving is out of the question.

Now you pull up to the ramp. Make sure that if you need a permit to use this particular ramp that you have already taken care of getting it. Assuming that there is not a line, try to pull in so that the boats stern is facing the ramp and the trailer and vehicle are straight. This may require that you pull up quite far from the ramp. My plan of attack now is to ready the boat for launching as rapidly as possible, so I do not hold up other boaters waiting to use the ramp. Take off the transom tie down strap and the motor support. Leave your outboard or outdrive tilted up so it will not get damaged if it accidentally hits the roadway. Most importantly, leave the winch strap or cable attached to the bow eye. This is one of the most common errors and failure to leave this secured can lead to a premature launching. This is usually onto the concrete ramp itself. This causes damage to the boat, great embarrassment and a long closure of the ramp. I tie dock lines to the bow and stern cleats on the side closest to the side of the ramp or dock where I will be launching. I bring the bowline forward and loop it around the winch post. This prevents the boat from drifting away from you when it first comes off the trailer.

I then return to the vehicle. If I have my family or guests with me they get out and watch from a safe distance. I once read a horrific story about a man who backed down the ramp and left his wife and two children in the car. He got out to launch his boat and somehow the car continued to move down the ramp. Whether the car jumped out of park, was left in neutral or the brakes failed, I did not hear. The car quickly became submerged with three people inside. A wild rescue ensued and all three were safely removed from the car. The important lesson is to leave everyone safely nearby, not in the vehicle.

When backing down the ramp, my preference is to look over my right shoulder and out of the back window of the vehicle. Just like when backing the boat, I need to keep this consistent. It makes it easier and it is the only way that I can do it. Using the side view mirrors is difficult for me. I had an extremely hard time keeping the trailer straight until I began looking over my right shoulder. Then, just like with docking, everything just fell into place. I began backing like a pro and no longer worried about doing it at all. Of course, practice makes perfect. Sometimes going to an empty parking lot and practicing backing straight can help a lot. The tow vehicle pushes the trailer back and the vehicle needs to follow in a series of small arcs to keep the trailer moving straight. Try to avoid exaggerated movements. Many people have learned to back a trailer using a technique which is really quite simple. The less that you think about it the better off you will be. Keep one hand at the bottom of the steering wheel in the six o'clock position. For a few minutes forget about right and left, it will only confuse you. Begin backing slowly. To get the trailer to move in the direction it needs to, just move your hand in that direction. When the trailer begins to move, it will be in the direction that you need it to. Then just follow it, correcting as you go. Getting back to right and left, to reiterate if you need the trailer to move right, move your hand right. This, because your hand is at the bottom of the steering wheel, is the equivalent of moving the wheel to the left. People swear by this technique. I guess it is just easier to think of things as the same. If you want to go to the right, just move your hand to the right. Same is good, I imagine. The rest requires practice to fully understand how moving the wheel will affect the trailer.

Once on the ramp itself I do my final straightening. Pulling ahead when necessary to get me close to the side of the ramp wall or dock. A helper to guide you back during this step is great. Every trailer is different, some require you to submerge the wheels and others do not. Of course, keeping the hubs out of the water is preferred, but not always possible. See what the manufacturer recommends, but do what you must to launch the boat easily. Stop the vehicle at the desired spot. I use the water depth on the tires as a gauge. This is figured out by trial and error. For vehicles with automatic transmissions, put the car in park, set the parking brake and shut the engine off. For vehicles with standard transmissions, put the car in gear, set the parking brake and shut the engine off. Carry a set of tire chocks and use them. Most people skip this step until they get a good scare. There is no need to wait until you experience a problem. Enough tow vehicles end up in the water each year to prove that this can actually happen. Learn from others mistakes and we will not repeat them.

At this point, we unhook the winch strap or cable and remove the safety chain from the bow eye. If your trailer has rollers and they are kept well oiled, the boat should roll right off and into the water. If you have bunks, or long pieces of carpeted wood, you may need to give it a little more than a gentle push to get it moving. If your bunks provide too much friction and make launching very difficult you have several options to make them work easier. You could line them with plastic strips which cut the friction or spray them with a product called "Liquid Rollers". It is an aerosol spray which decreases the friction as well. I know some people who simply put dish detergent on them. Now that the boat is coming off the trailer so well, you will appreciate the dock line that you have wrapped around your winch post. Use this line, as well as your pre rigged stern line to guide your boat to your desired location and tie it off. Make sure that it is out of other peoples way as much as possible. Then pull your vehicle off the ramp, do not forget your tire chocks. Most ramps provide ample parking. Make sure that you plan ahead and try not to take a spot where you can be blocked in or otherwise denied direct access back to the ramp.

A few more things need to be mentioned about the ramp itself. All ramps, no mater where you are, end somewhere. At low tide, the end of the ramp may be closer than you think. This means that if you back down too far, the trailer tires can drop off of the end of the concrete. They may begin to sink into the sand and mud. Most ramps, where this is a risk, will mark the sides of the ramp with a line of paint. One ramp which I use quite often has a piece of PVC pipe that sticks up on each side for just this reason.

You must look for these markers and realize what they signify. If you do happen to fall off the end of the ramp, the best thing to do is to launch the boat from the trailer to rid it of extra weight. Then pull forward in low gear or 4WD if you have it. Sometimes you may need a person or two in the water to help lift the end of the trailer as you pull forward. Many ramps have been modernized or improved in recent years to avoid this problem. Be leery and look for any significant markings. A little local knowledge helps a lot in these situations. Do not be afraid to ask others who are launching or in a local bait shop. People are usually eager to offer assistance. One more item concerning ramps, mostly at low tide, algae or seaweed may have accumulated on the ramp. It can cause you to slip and fall. Usually you are most vulnerable when you hop out of your vehicle. You are most impressed with the great job you have done backing down the ramp and all of the gawkers think you are a pro. You hop out and land on your duff. Funny, but also dangerous, not to mention embarrassing. In addition, the same problem can affect your vehicle. It can slip seaward very easily. It also can make pulling back up the ramp very difficult. Four wheel drive can come in very handy in this situation, but basically, if the ramp is slick, the ramp is slick. You may need to wait until a higher tide to haul your boat. Ice can cause the same problems if you boat in winter. Be aware and be careful.

Once your vehicle is parked and locked, go do what you came here to do. Enjoy a day on the water. When your vehicle and trailer are at the ramp, people have a good idea that you are not around. So for piece of mind, lock not only your vehicle but secure your trailer to the hitch as well. If you have an insert that fits into a hitch receiver, you should lock that also.

I remember the theft of a trailer from a local ramp which was attributed to this omission. It is very easy to slip the insert out of its receptacle and into the receiver on another vehicle. Fortunately, you can purchase a locking pin to act as a deterrent and solve this problem. One of my biggest fears is boating in some remote location only to find your trailer missing upon your return. Thankfully, you do not hear of that sort of thing too often. It would truly be a nightmare if it were to happen. This is one thing that I cannot teach you to be fully prepared for. Lock everything, avoid seedy looking locations and do not worry about it enough so that it ruins your day.

Returning to the ramp requires a process much like launching, but in reverse. Pre rig the dock lines and tie off to the side of the ramp. Tilt the engine all the way up. When I go to get my truck and trailer, I stop off at the trailer and pull the winch strap or cable all the way down to the axle and hang the hook somewhere on the trailer. You will see why later. Pull out of your parking spot and align the trailer with the ramp. Now you will see that a new problem is at hand. It is very difficult to see the trailer from the vehicle without the boat on it. If you cannot see it, then you do not know where it is and therefore you cannot back it straight. If you have a rear hatch or anything in the vehicle which can be opened to provide you with visual access, do so. I have a pickup truck and make sure that the tailgate can be put down with every trailer that I use. This allows me to see the entire trailer. If there is no way that you can see the trailer from your vehicle, then you can attach poles or flags to the trailer which lets you know where it is.

Back down the ramp and submerge the tires to the same level that you did when launching. Shut down the vehicle, set the parking brake as described before and put your tire chocks in place. Use your dock lines to bring the boat to the trailer. When close to the trailer you can easily attach the pre-positioned winch hook to the bow eye. This can be done by leaning over the boats bow or leaning over from the side of the ramp. Either way it is simple, as the hook is in the right place and at the ready when you need it. Keep a good hold on the bow line and use it to keep the boat in position as you make your way forward to the winch. Begin to take up the slack with the winch. The use of Guide Ons helps a great deal with this step.

As stated previously, they are quite simply vertical poles or portions of trailer bunks. They rest against the boats hull and do just what their name implies. They guide the boat onto the trailer, accurately positioning it as it is drawn up with the winch. If you do not have Guide Ons, you need to check hull position and adjust port and starboard as you winch it in. An electric winch is a great aid as well. It saves your arms and back and does all the work with the push of a button. One word of caution with electric winches is that you may need to leave the tow vehicles engine running while using the winch. Otherwise, the battery may be drained. Due to this, tire chocks become a definite necessity.

With the boat fully winched up, reattach the safety chain from the winch post to the bow eye. Stow all the lines onboard and gently pull the vehicle forward. Once you are out of the launching area directly, then stow your gear, place your transom strap, motor support etc. At some point you should wash the trailer off thoroughly with fresh water. We all need to be increasingly concerned with cross contamination of various forms of aquatic life between boating venues. Here in the Northeast we have a problem with Zebra Mussels. They are rapidly making their way from lake to lake, raising concern about their impact upon these ecosystems. They are a very hardy species which competes for food with native life and also clogs underwater plumbing creating a great number of problems. It is thought that they are carried on boat trailers, in bilge water or on the motors or hulls of boats that have spent time in infested waters. Maine recently enacted some strong legislation regarding the transport of invasive aquatic plants. You can be fined up to $500 if your trailer has any aquatic plants hanging off of it. This is necessary to avoid contamination of Maine's lakes and ponds with various forms of vegetation which will rob the native plants of sunlight and destroy their fragile ecosystem. Be sure to wash the wheels, axle and lights to keep them from corroding, but also to prevent this problem. Some other general maintenance, aside from what was already discussed, is to take care of any rust or corrosion that develops. Sand these spots down to bare metal and spray paint them with either paint or liquid galvanizing, depending upon your trailers finish. Oil the rollers regularly and basically keep an eye out for any components that may be exhibiting wear or need updating.

When winter comes, the trailer should be jacked up off of the ground and blocked. This takes the weight of the boat off of the trailers springs and tires. It is also good for the tires to be off of the ground. This will help to prevent dry rot. Also, cover the tires with shades when possible, to protect them from UV radiation. Check the tires for signs of UV damage from this by looking at the sidewalls for cracks in the rubber.

As stated earlier, the trailer is just another piece of gear. It needs to be understood, be used and maintained properly. With this proper use and care, it will provide you with many years of service. The trailer is a means by which we accomplish our end. The end, of course is to spend time on the water. We must slightly redefine our goals however. As a trailer boater, we no longer only want to get back to the dock safely, we want to get the boat and our family all the way back home safely.

Chapter 10

CONCLUSION

*The secret of success is constancy
to purpose.*
—*Benjamin Franklin*

Congratulations!! It is evident that by getting to this portion of the book that you are willing to learn and not too arrogant to think that this book is beneath your level of expertise. This being a book for beginning boaters, some things we have discussed have been quite basic. As with anything in life we need to be open to learning. It is my hope that some of you have learned a huge amount. While others may have learned far less, any new knowledge gained is a gift.

This book has touched on so many aspects of boating and intentionally avoided quite a few. I feel that the basics are the most important because without that sound foundation everything else we learn will be on shaky ground. My advice is to read everything you can get your hands on. From small publications to magazines to textbooks. I keep a library of reading material and like to look over books that I have previously read, to keep concepts fresh in my mind. Secondly, get out and go. Practice is critical and paramount to success. Be careful to not push yourself beyond your limit or the limit of your boat, but do not prevent yourself from advancing. Try different things, go farther, plan that short cruise and overnight stay. Finally, live the boating life. Bring a little bit of your hobby into your everyday life, even if it is just reading a boating magazine at lunchtime, stealing a few minutes out of your day to browse through a boating store or take a break from the grind and visit the web site of a future cruising destination. Remember, boating is what we do in the summer. Planning and learning is what we do in the winter. For those of you fortunate enough to live in a climate where boating can be enjoyed year round, do your planning and reading on rainy days.

I keep a three foot section of three strand line in my office and during times of stress, I practice tying knots. It immediately cools me down. My work life revolves around keeping a schedule down to the minute. My wife bought me a Tidal Chronometer, a wristwatch that also tells you the state of the tide. Every few minutes when I refer to it, I feel my blood pressure drop a bit. I visit the Tidal Fish message boards on the Internet several times a day to take me away from reality for a few minutes and keep me updated on where the fish are. I have joined several environmental organizations such as the Chesapeake Bay Foundation and thoroughly enjoy reading their newsletters when they arrive. I tinker with my boats regularly adding, enhancing and repairing whatever I can. I am a member of the Antique Outboard Motor Club, which combines my passions of all things nautical, antiques and fixing mechanical things. I enjoy building wooden skiffs, classically styled dinghies and small wood boats of all kinds. This brings boating down to a more fundamental level for me. Am I obsessed? Nah, just passionate. It is my only vice and I do not let it interfere with my family life, which is truly the most important thing to me. What it does is offer me a diversion from the incredible stress of the day to make me calmer during my off hours. This, in a nutshell, is the reason why I do what I do.

However you chose to enjoy your hobby, whether you cruise from Nantucket to the Bahamas in a 50' trawler or stay within a mile of your home port in a 14' skiff, do it safely and do it well. Preparedness is the key to safe boating and troubleshooting potential problems. All of the tools and equipment in the world however, will do no good without the knowledge to use them properly. The safety of you and your passengers is and must remain the overriding issue in whatever you do. To help keep things clear, you must focus on any problems that may arise with a calm head. Problems unfortunately arise quite often on the water. The knowledgeable, self confident boater will do well. Deal with the problem and move on. Others may not be so lucky. Their problems may cause damage to their boat, cost them money or worse. The knowledge, confidence and high level of preparedness that you gain from books like this, will be invaluable in your time of need.

By completing this book you have entered into an elite group of responsible boaters. Very few boaters actually read books on the subject. Go one step further. Keep it handy and refer to it often. Strive to achieve a higher level of freedom through your hobby and play safe.

Appendix

Accuweather
www.accuweather.com

Bluewater Cruising Guides
1-800-942-2583

Boat/US Foundation
880 South Pickett Street
Alexandria, VA 22304-4606
1-703-823-9550
Membership 1-800-395-2628
www.boatus.com

Chart Kit Books—Maptech
1-888-839-5551
www.maptech.com

Cruising Guide Publications
1-800-330-9542

Earthwatch Weather
www.earthwatch.com

National Fire Protection Association
1 Batterymarch Park
Quincy, MA 02269-9101
1-617-770-3000

National Data Buoy Center
www.ndbc.noaa.gov

National Weather Service
www.nws.gov

NOAA Distribution Service
National Ocean Service
Riverdale, MD 20737-01199
1-800-638-8972
http://acc.nos.noaa.gov
For Chart Number One, Coast Pilots and others

NOAA National Weather Service
www.nws.noaa.gov

U.S. Coast Guard Auxiliary
www.cgaux.org

United States Coast Guard Headquarters
2100 Second Street, SW,
Washington, DC 20593
General Information: 1-202-267-2229
www.uscg.mil

U.S. Coast Guard Recreational Boating Safety Program
1-800-368-5647
infoline@navcen.uscg.mil
www.uscgboating.org

U.S. Coast Guard Navigation Center
7323 Telegraph Road
Alexandria, VA 22310
1-703-313-5800
www.navcen.uscg.mil
For Local Notice to Mariners information
contact your local Coast Guard District, go to
Coast Guard Headquarters page for links.

U.S. Coast Guard SOS
For Maritime Search and Rescue Emergencies
For the Great Lakes, Gulf and East Coast:
Atlantic Area Command Center: 1-757-398-0631
For the Hawaiian, Alaskan and Pacific Coast:
Pacific Area Command Center: 1-510-437-3701

U.S. Government Printing Office (GPO)
Superintendent of Documents
Washington, DC 20402
For Light Lists, Rules of the Road
1-202-512-1800

Waterway Guide Series
1-800-941-2219

Printed in the United States
44037LVS00001B/10